THE FALAISE POCKET
NORMANDY, AUGUST 1944

CASEMATE | ILLUSTRATED

CASEMATE | ILLUSTRATED

THE FALAISE POCKET

NORMANDY, AUGUST 1944

YVES BUFFETAUT

CASEMATE | ILLUSTRATED

MILITARIA

CIS0010

Print Edition: ISBN 978-1-61200-7274
Digital Edition: ISBN 978-1-61200-7281

This book is published in cooperation with and under license from Sophia Histoire & Collections. Originally published in French as Militaria Hors-Serie No 46,
Translation by Hannah McAdams
Design by Mary Woolley, Battlefield Design
Color artwork by Jean Restayn © Histoire & Collections
Infographics by Leonie Young and Denis Gillé
Additional text by Chris Cocks
Photo retouching and separations by Remy Spezzano
Printed and bound by Megaprint, Turkey

CASEMATE PUBLISHERS (US)
Telephone (610) 853-9131
Fax (610) 853-9146
Email: casemate@casematepublishers.com
www.casematepublishers.com

CASEMATE PUBLISHERS (UK)
Telephone (01865) 241249
Fax (01865) 794449
Email: casemate-uk@casematepublishers.co.uk
www.casematepublishers.co.uk

Title page: The bulk of the panzer divisions had generally fought against the British, and when the Americans succeeded in breaking through, the Germans could not disengage quickly enough to counterattack with any significant force. The Mortain counteroffensive only employed three panzer divisions, just one of which was fresh: the 116th Panzer Division. Tigers from the heavy battalions, like these from the 102nd SS Heavy Panzer Battalion, remained on the British front. (ECPAD)
Contents page: Young Hohenstaufen Division troops scan the sky for Allied "Jabos." (ECPAD)
Map: The Western Front, August 7–11, 1944

Note: vehicle illustrations and profiles are not to scale.

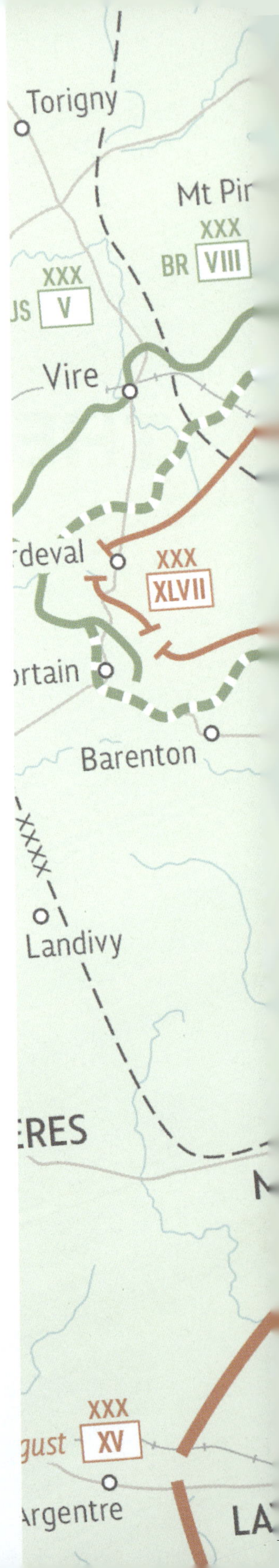

A 3.7-inch gun in action in August 1944, during the battle of the Falaise Pocket. This piece with a caliber of just over 92mm was the equivalent of a German 8.8cm gun. (IWM B9227)

AUGUST

August 4, 1944: Allies capture Rennes, and prepare to close the Falaise–Argentan Pocket.

August 7, 1944: Von Kluge launches Operation *Lüttich*, from Mortain to Avranches, to cut off Patton's Third Army. Allied Typhoons and Thunderbolts destroy 116 panzers and as many armored vehicles.

August 8, 1944: Operation *Lüttich*—that sees the bloodiest fighting of the Normandy campaign—fails. Troops of the U.S. Third Army capture Le Mans, formerly the German 7th Army headquarters.

Montgomery orders U.S. First and Third Armies, British Second Army and Canadian First Army to converge on Falaise–Chambois area to commence encirclement of Army Group B.

August 17, 1944: Germans begin withdrawing.

August 19, 1944: Allies link up at Chambois but German counterattacks force gaps in the Allied lines, allowing thousands of Germans to escape.

August 21, 1944: The Falaise Pocket is sealed. Some 60,000 Germans are trapped and neutralized, along with 500 tanks and assault guns destroyed.

August 30, 1944: Remnants of Army Group B retreat across the Seine, Paris is liberated and the Normandy campaign officially ends.

The German Army after the Defeat at Mortain

While the failure at Mortain was not overly costly for the German army, the American breakthrough and subsequent rapid advance through the region provoked a clear shift in the German defensive strategy in the west.

For the first time since the Normandy landings of June 1944, Hitler began to consider abandoning France, or at least Normandy. He knew that the River Seine, with its many meanders, was not tenable as a defensive position. It could only serve as a checkpoint, in any event requiring a large number of men to hold it. But the Seine was not the only natural barrier between Normandy and the German frontier. General Alfred Jodl, Chief of Staff

A Tiger from the 102nd SS Heavy Panzer Battalion at the front in the Caen sector. In order to operate effectively in the west, the 7th Army had to be sure that Eberbach's 5th Panzer Army could contain the British. (ECPAD)

The population of Normandy was the real victim of the battle that began on June 6: towns and villages were destroyed, large numbers of civilians were killed, and livestock was slaughtered wholesale. This photo, taken either in the southern Calvados region or in La Manche, shows a Panzer IV from an unidentified unit behind fleeing civilians. (ECPAD)

of Oberkommando des Heeres (OKH, or Army High Command) began preparing a long defensive barrier, comprised of two principal lines: the first ran from the English Channel to the Vosges Mountains via a series of rivers—the Somme, the Marne and the Saône—while the second, closer to Germany, curved through the Albert Canal and the Meuse before also reaching the Vosges. This was the Siegfried Line; its fortifications had been neglected for the past four years in favor of the Atlantic Wall, but it remained a formidable line of defense. Toward the end of July, Jodl began repairing the line through Organization Todt, requisitioning Belgian and French civilians, essentially slave labor, to work on the defenses along the roads and rivers.

On July 31, Hitler made two important decisions, one of which had an immediate effect: the Allies were to be prevented from using any French ports, which meant that in Brittany the Germans were obliged to concentrate their forces around the ports and consequently abandon the interior. A similar outcome, that is the abandoning of the hinterland, would have occurred anyway had the Western Front collapsed, along with the requisite destruction of all road and railway infrastructure that would have accompanied a retreat. The other, equally fateful decision was to launch Operation *Lüttich*.

Organization Todt (OT) was formed in 1933 as a vast engineering operation across the Third Reich. It was named after its founder, Fritz Todt, who was responsible for developing the national infrastructure, including the rail and autobahn networks. Todt died in an aircraft crash in 1942 and was succeeded by the mercurial Albert Speer, the Minister of Armaments and Munitions. OT employed some 1.4 million slave laborers.

The omnipresence of Allied fighter-bombers, referred to as "Jabos" by the Germans, was a constant thorn in the side of the Wehrmacht, preventing them from carrying out any maneuvers during the day. The Flak that accompanied all armored units was insufficient to repel the Typhoons and Thunderbolts. This Flakvierling from the 12th SS Panzer Division Hitlerjugend, photographed at the end of July, boasts seven kills since June 8, 1944: two Mustangs, a Spitfire, three Typhoons (the last shot down on July 25) and a Thunderbolt. (ECPAD)

The Western Front is Not Lost

Even after the Americans had broken through at Avranches, the situation in Normandy was not completely desperate. The arrival of General George Patton's Third Army in Brittany was not as critical as it was first painted to be: it would be some time before Patton would be able to make any impact against the Western Front proper. Hitler was right, therefore, to hang on to Normandy, as it was the shortest front he could hope for in the west. At the same time, however, if the Germans were unable to rapidly consolidate and stabilize themselves after their spectacular breakthroughs made during *Cobra*, they would find themselves in an extremely invidious position, subjected to superior Allied air power that would critically hamper the panzers' war of movement.

According to the war diary of Oberkommando der Wehrmacht (OKW, or High Command of the Armed Forces), the situation in Normandy by July 30 was critical, but not hopeless. It was now more than apparent that the Allies were not going to open a second front in the west by landing at the Pas-de-Calais: thus, the arrival of Canadian divisions in Normandy demonstrated that Patton's supposed army corps in England did not exist, and neither did the vast numbers of supposed ground-attack aircraft in Normandy.

In addition, the American breakthrough in Brittany rendered any further landing pointless, as the Allies had finally managed to transition from static to mobile warfare. In many respects, and almost perversely, knowing that they were already facing the entire Allied invasion force was something of a relief for the Wehrmacht. Being aware of what they were up against allowed the German commanders to release forces from defensive stop-gaps that were now redundant and shift them to the front lines.

No Retreat

For Hitler, to retreat and abandon Normandy while the front was still intact was unthinkable, as the army would certainly lose a large amount of its matériel and the only short, tenable front thereafter would be one of Jodl's river lines or the Siegfried Line itself. Politically and strategically, Hitler simply could not relinquish Normandy.

On August 1, while Field Marshal Günther von Kluge was preparing to launch a counterattack on Mortain, significant German reinforcements—one armored division and six infantry divisions—were en route to Normandy.

An SPW column of SdKfz 251 Ds passes through an as-yet-undamaged village at the end of July 1944. The vehicles are well camouflaged, protection against Allied air power. (ECPAD)

The 84th and 85th Infantry Divisions were on their way from the Pas-de-Calais. The 89th Infantry Division had just crossed the Seine, while the 331st Infantry Division was just about to do so. Elsewhere, elements of the 363rd Infantry Division were crossing the Loire near Angers, and the 9th Panzer Division was approaching the same river, where it would regroup at Alençon.

This panzer division was almost at full strength, as the two battalions of the 33rd Panzer Regiment had 78 Panzer IVs and 79 Panthers respectively, supported by eight 37mm Flakpanzer IVs.

Outside Avranches, the situation was not wholly unfavorable for the Germans. The 5th Panzer Group West, renamed the 4th Army on August 5, was managing to contain the British with some of its elements even reporting a quiet front. Only II Panzer Corps was under pressure from Montgomery's advance against Vire, but even there the front held firm.

The 7th Army was, however, under threat from the American advance. The attack launched by von Kluge towards Avranches on August 6 had not succeeded and this would have serious consequences. But this failure was not the only cause, or even the most important cause, of Germany's ultimate collapse in Normandy.

American soldiers from the First Army take a break in the cellar of a wine or cider merchant in Tessy-sur-Vire, August 3, 1944. The American advance on Vire was facilitated by the withdrawal ordered by Hitler in order to free up troops for Operation *Lüttich*. (DITE/USIS)

Bundesarchiv, Bild 183-2004-0524-500 / CC-BY-SA 3.0

In Profile:
Field Marshal Günther von Kluge

Günther von Kluge was born Günther Adolf Ferdinand Kluge on October 30, 1882, to a military family in Posen, Prussia. In 1901, von Kluge was commissioned into the Prussian 46th Field Artillery Regiment, serving on the General Staff between 1910 and 1918. On the Western Front, he attained the rank of captain. He stayed on in the army after the armistice, being promoted to lieutenant-general commanding the 6th Division in 1934. With the establishment of the Wehrmacht in 1935, von Kluge was promoted again, to VI Corps, then 6th Army Group and the 4th Army which took part in the invasion of Poland in 1939.

Von Kluge's 4th Army was then transferred to Gerd von Rundstedt's Army Group A for the invasion of France where, together with Erwin Rommel, he was responsible for the successful blitzkrieg that overwhelmed France and the Low Countries. In July 1940 he was promoted to field marshal. Von Kluge and his 4th Army then participated in Operation *Barbarossa*, the invasion of the Soviet Union. He was to take over Army Group Center from von Bock before being involved in a serious car accident on the Minsk–Smolensk road in October 1943. He was only able to return to duty in July 1944 as commander of the German forces in the West (Oberbefehlshaber West)

Von Kluge had little respect for the Nazis and what he called Hitler's "crude militarism," however he took immense pride in German rearmament and the rise of the Wehrmacht. Probably not an active plotter in the July 20 assassination attempt on Hitler, he was undoubtedly aware of it. Recalled to Berlin in the aftermath of the plot, he committed suicide on August 19, his suicide note urging Hitler to display "the greatness that will be needed to put an end to a hopeless struggle." There is a suggestion that von Kluge was shot in the head by Jürgen Stroop after refusing to swallow the potassium cyanide pill handed him.

A Tiger from the 102nd SS Heavy Panzer Battalion in the *bocage*. The hedgerows gave the German defenders a distinct advantage, but even on the plains, as at Caen, the Germans were capable of slowing or stopping British offensives. (ECPAD)

Overlord Revisited

According to the initial plans for Operation *Overlord*, the American effort was to be directed toward Brittany, unless the German front collapsed or the Germans chose to retreat. Over the first few days of August, it appeared that this plan needed little modification, as the Germans were holding firm everywhere except in Brittany. But the events at Mortain changed all that. For the first time, the Allies considered a new possibility: that of no longer prioritizing the liberation of Brittany, and instead concentrating on a rapid advance towards the two principal ports on the Seine: Le Havre and Rouen. Ironically, Montgomery had suggested this before Operation *Cobra* and had reiterated it after the breakthrough at Avranches.

SHAEF, the Supreme Headquarters Allied Expeditionary Force, was formed in December 1943 under General Dwight D. Eisenhower, after his transfer from the Mediterranean Theater of Operations. SHAEF's raison d'être was Operation *Overlord*, and the invasion of Northwestern Europe. It comprised three army groups controlling eight field armies, two tactical air forces and considerable naval resources.

On July 29, Supreme Headquarters Allied Expeditionary Force (SHAEF) decided that it would be possible for one sole American corps (an armored division and three divisions) to "finish the conquest" of Brittany. This implies that the U.S. Third Army would be freed up for other operations: surrounding the Germans to the west of the Seine, luring them away from the river and then crushing them, in preparation for the ultimate effort of an Allied march on Paris and crossing the river themselves.

An infantryman from the 16th Luftwaffe Field Division waits for the enemy to arrive on the plains at Caen. This division was almost annihilated during the bombing of Caen on July 7, 1944, and then finally finished off as a unit during Operation *Goodwood* on July 18. A few survivors carried on fighting in occasional *kampfgruppen*, or battle groups, as encountered by the British in the aftermath of the battle of the Falaise Pocket. (ECPAD)

Lieutenant Thompson from Englewood, New Jersey, uses a field telephone at a company command post. Next to him is an M1 Garand and two walkie-talkie radios. This photo was taken near Saint-Barthélémy during the German counteroffensive on Mortain; Saint-Barthélémy is 5 kilometers from Mortain in the sector held by the U.S. 30th Infantry Division. (DITE/USIS)

An American armored column passes a group of cheering residents at Saint-Pois. During the battle of Mortain, Saint-Pois was in the sector held by the U.S. 4th Infantry Division, with the 3rd Armored Division in support. (DITE/USIS)

Near Barenton, two American soldiers examine an 8.8cm Flak gun that has been sabotaged and abandoned. These men are most likely from Combat Command A, 3rd Armored Division. The presence of this division on the German left flank would prove bothersome for von Kluge. (DITE/USIS)

An American infantry column advances toward Sourdeval after the German defeat at Mortain. It was the 28th U.S. Division, XVIII Corps that entered the town, so it is safe to assume that this column belongs to the same. (DITE/USIS)

On August 2, General Eisenhower, the supreme Allied commander, determined that General Omar Bradley had literally "opened the German left flank," and decided that the Allies were now free to strike where they wished, that is to say, more eastward than to the west.

The Americans had made substantial progress in the west of France. As far as Brittany was concerned, Vannes was liberated on August 5, as was Redon, and by August 6 the 6th Armored Division had arrived at Lesneven, just 20 kilometers from Brest. While it is true that the latter only fell in September after a fierce battle, and the Lorient and Saint-Nazaire pockets held on until May 1945, Brittany had been almost completely liberated even before the German counterattack at Mortain, and, moreover, any Germans left in the area were not in a position to pose any kind of threat.

However, the American situation farther east—where several German divisions in Normandy had found themselves surrounded—was arguably more interesting. The entire German front had contracted when Hitler had ordered the shortening of the lines to free up certain units for von Kluge's counterattack. That's not to say that the German force was necessarily weakened; in fact, it was more solid than ever, both south of Caen and Vire, and from Saint-Pois to Mortain. South of Mortain, however, was a figurative gulf: the Germans had nothing with which to oppose Patton's divisions, and the U.S. XV Corps had already reached Mayenne, Laval and Chateau-Gontier. Some units had even arrived at Sainte-Suzanne, less than 40 kilometers from Le Mans.

The curate of Château-Gontier welcomes soldiers from XVIII Corps on August 6, 1944. The M-5 Stuart belongs to the 5th Armored Division of Patton's Third Army. The presence of American troops so far east posed a serious threat to the Germans fighting in Normandy. (DITE/USIS)

An American M-10 in action in the Barenton sector on August 5, 1944. The crew scans the skies for enemy aircraft, and the tank destroyer is carefully camouflaged, a necessity in hedgerow warfare. As for the Luftwaffe, it was heavily involved in supporting the Mortain offensive, but over 300 aircraft were intercepted by Allied aviation long before they arrived on target. (DITE/USIS)

An SdKfz 251 D from the 12th SS Panzer Division Hitlerjugend, which fought against the British. (ECPAD)

Can the Germans Reduce the Corridor?

Operation *Lüttich* was launched shortly after midnight on August 7, the panzers advancing under the cover of darkness without difficulty. The ease of movement over the first few hours instilled the Germans with confidence, and they advanced several kilometers: the 2nd SS Panzer Division Das Reich travelled along the Sélune, through Milly, Poirier, and Fontenay. The 2nd Panzer Division did slightly better by advancing as far as Le Mesnil-Adelée. However, to its right, the 116th Panzer Division was making little headway, and, to its left, the progress of the 1st SS Panzer Division Leibstandarte SS Adolf Hitler (LSSAH) north of Mortain was painfully slow. It should be noted that the terrain was particularly ill suited to tanks, favoring a static defense.

By late morning, the fog that covered the hillsides had dissipated and brilliant sunlight marked an end to the first phase of the offensive. Allied aircraft attacked in force, while the Luftwaffe, grounded in the Paris region or engaged in aerial combat away from the front, was powerless to intervene. Over a few hours, the German attack foundered under wave upon wave of Hawker Typhoons and P-47 Thunderbolts. This is widely acknowledged as the first time an offensive was halted by the force of air power alone.

Forced to hide out in groves of trees, behind hedges and along sunken roads, the panzers were unable to progress. The panzergrenadiers were no better off. By the end of the day, Allied pilots had destroyed over 110 tanks and as many armored vehicles. These figures are probably exaggerated, but they do give an indication of German losses.

On August 8, the panzer attack came to a complete halt. Four companies of the U.S. 102nd Infantry Regiment held Hill 307 to the east of Mortain, significantly hindering the movement of German troops in the sector. The Das Reich could not dislodge them. Elsewhere, the 2nd Panzer Division was the only armored division to attempt to continue its advance; it was quickly stopped by Allied aircraft.

During the night of August 7/8, 1944, just 24 hours after the start of Operation *Lüttich*, the 5th Panzer Army's front line was shaken by a massive air raid south of Caen. This was the commencement of Operation *Totalize*, which struck approximately 5 kilometers south of Caen along the Caen–Falaise road. The Germans estimated that around 600 Canadian tanks had arrived, posing such a threat that any reprise of the German offensive on Avranches was considered futile. The decision whether or not to abandon Operation *Lüttich* thus fell to von Kluge.

XATIVE

Tanks from the U.S. 3rd Armored Division open fire on German positions near Barenton on August 5, 1944. The "Laxative" in the foreground is an M-8 that fired 75mm "suppositories." Behind it is a Sherman M4-A1 76mm, the most powerful tank in the American line-up at the time. The 76mm cannon was, however, clearly less effective than the 17-pounder on the British Firefly. (DITE/USIS)

A U.S. Eighth Air Force Republic P-47D-22-RE Thunderbolt (s/n 42-25969) in flight. It was lost on August 3, 1944 while assigned to the 56th Fighter Group/63rd Fighter Squadron; the pilot Lieutenant Roach Stewart Jr was KIA. (USAF)

In Profile: "Jabos"

"Jabo," short for *jagdbomber*, meaning literally a fighter- or hunter-bomber, and the German infantryman's nickname for the aircraft became a significant feature of World War II. An integral part of the German *blitzkrieg* tactics during the invasions of Poland, and then the Low Countries and France, the Junkers 87—or Stuka, from *sturzkampfflugzeug*, meaning "dive bomber"—was a German dive bomber and ground-attack aircraft. It first saw action with the Luftwaffe's Condor Legion during the Spanish Civil War, achieving notoriety for its role in the 1937 bombing atrocity of the Basque town of Guernica: its siren, which was switched on during its near-vertical bombing run, came to symbolize the terror it instilled. (Interestingly, the first aerial kill of the war, on September 1, 1939, is credited to Stuka pilot Unteroffizier Frank Neuber who shot down—over Balice after a raid on Rakowice aerodrome—Captain M. Medwecki, the CO of Polish III/2 Fighter Wing, flying a PZL P.11 fighter aircraft.)

But any fighter that could carry a bomb could adopt a fighter-bomber role: from RAF Spitfires and Hurricanes to Luftwaffe Messerschmitt Bf 109s. The Luftwaffe was soon to convert the Focke-Wulf 190 fighter version to the super-fast Fw 190 A-3/U3 "Jabo" that successfully conducted several raids against English coastal towns. During World War II, the Japanese were perhaps the first to successfully utilize dive-bombers—and torpedo-carrier bombers (such as the Nakajima B5N "Kate")—in that specific role, all principally carrier-borne. It was the squadrons of carrier-borne Mitsubishi A6M "Zeros" and Aichi D3A "Vals" that wreaked such havoc at Pearl Harbor.

But it was on the Eastern Front, after the Wehrmacht began their long, slow retreat from Stalingrad, that the term "Jabo" came to assume the frightening connotations it did for the German troops. It was the Soviets' lumbering IL-2 Sturmovik "flying tank"—like the T-34 tank mass-produced in such vast quantities—that simply swamped the beleaguered Luftwaffe by its sheer weight of numbers and was able to inflict such devastation on, and instill such fear in, the German armies on the steppes of Russia and the Ukraine. Thus it was, by definition and reputation, that the RAF's Hawker Typhoons and the U.S. Eighth Air Force's Republic P-47 Thunderbolts were able to so clinically adopt the "Jabo" mantle in Normandy.

A Junkers Ju 87 D-5 "Stuka" on the Finnish front, June 1944, about to take off. (SA-kuva / Eino Nurmi)

A pilot of 175 Squadron, RAF, scrambles to his waiting Hawker Typhoon Mk IB fighter-bomber at Le Fresne-Camilly in Normandy, July 24, 1944. (IWM CL 570 / F/O N. S. Clark RAF)

Elements of the 15th Scottish Division at Moncharivel on August 5, 1944. The AFV is an M-10 tank destroyer. (IWM B8645)

British Pressure on the North of the Front

On August 6, 1944, the Americans seized Vire and the British began the assault on Mont Pinçon, a key position on the German front.

Mont Pinçon was not some insurmountable peak as its name "pincer" may suggest; it is only 1,300 feet high, but its slopes, especially those facing west, are very steep and were a real obstacle to the British on their way south.

During the battle of Villers-Bocage in June 1944, the Tigers of the 101st SS Heavy Panzer Battalion distinguished themselves by stopping an audacious maneuver attempted by the British 7th Armoured Division, with Obersturmführer Wittmann playing a pivotal role. These Tigers were used during the fight over Villers-Bocage, and the British infantry put in six solid hours of combat, as did the Panzer IVs of the Panzer Lehr Division. This photograph, taken in early August, shows two destroyed Tigers in the ruins of a liberated town. (IWM B8635)

South of the village of Evrecy, the Germans placed batteries of 8.8cm guns along the left bank of the Orne, which stopped or frustrated any British offensives. This battery, however, was captured in early August 1944. (IWM B8665)

Mont Pinçon was well defended by the Germans, and on its ultimate capture the British recovered important enemy matériel, including Pak 40 antitank artillery pieces. (IWM B9226)

German prisoners of war file past a Hummel destroyed in the village of Plessis-Grimoult on the left bank of the Orne. (IWM B8874)

At midday on August 6, two battalions of the British 129th Brigade, 43rd Division joined the tanks from the 13/18th Hussars on the banks of the Druance, where they waited for the start of the artillery barrage. This began with smoke canisters, which provided cover for the engineers to clear the ground of mines sown by the Germans. The 5th Wiltshire Battalion began crossing the river, but had not reached the opposite bank when enemy machine guns and mortars opened fire. Within minutes, the two leading companies were reduced to chaos, with dozens of men cut down. The regimental commander tried to regroup the men, but he too was killed, and the attack stalled. Several hundred meters north, the 4th Battalion of the Somerset Light Infantry was in similar trouble, its supporting tanks stopped in their tracks by mines, and the infantry pinned down.

Approaching the Summit of Mont Pinçon

The one slim hope of success rested in the bridge at La Varinière, over the Le Parc au Céne stream, that had been cleared of mines by Allied engineers, which allowed two Shermans from the 13/18th Hussars to cross. These tanks then fired on the Germans in the neighboring orchards, clearing the way for six more Shermans and 60 Wiltshire infantrymen to cross the bridge. Within 20 minutes, they had taken and secured the crossing.

After a short break, the troops discovered a dirt road that seemed to lead right to the top of Mont Pinçon. A little after 1800 hours, the tanks began the ascent, but the path was so steep and craggy that one tank overturned and fell into a quarry, and another was destroyed by the Germans. The remaining tanks managed to reach the top of the hill, where they caused considerable confusion among the ranks of Germans stationed there. From below, the brigade commander watched the tanks advance and ordered his reserves, the 4th Wiltshire Battalion, to follow them to the summit as quickly as possible.

This battalion was already exhausted and much reduced from the previous day's fighting, but despite its heavy losses, it was forced to effect an exhausting climb at night under a rain of German shells. Major Parsons, a company commander, recalls the attack:

> Enemy resistance was slight and the chief difficulty was the physical effort of climbing, for the slope soon became very steep and covered with scrub … The sergeant, commanding the leading platoon, very resourcefully told his men that they were not doing an attack, but were going up to relieve another unit already there. This materially helped the speed of the advance … As we neared the top a thick fog came down. We could see no landmarks but we found the tanks. They were relieved to see us, for Germans could be heard shouting and digging in close by. We were as tired as any troops could be, and many of us fell asleep as we were digging positions in the rocky soil, falling headlong pick in hand into the half-dug trenches, "dead to the world."

British soldiers examine a Brummbär, an unusual German tank armed with a 15cm howitzer and built on the chassis of a Panzer IV. This photograph was taken at Ondefontaine on August 6, 1944. Just one sturmpanzer unit was still operational in Normandy at this time: the 217th Sturmpanzer Battalion, which arrived at the front in July. (IWM B8738)

American troops arrive at Vire on August 7, 1944. Like Villers-Bocage and Lisieux, the town has been utterly reduced to rubble. (DITE/USIS)

The Canadians Prepare for Operation *Totalize*

Changes in the German troop dispositions for Operation *Lüttich* had materially altered the appearance of the front south of Caen by the beginning of August. The most formidable units, notably the 1st SS Panzer Division Leibstandarte SS Adolf Hitler and the 9th SS Panzer Division Hohenstaufen gave way to two infantry divisions, with the only mobile reserve left for General Sepp Dietrich's I SS Panzer Corps being the 12th SS Panzer Division Hitlerjugend, with around 50 tanks. However, the antitank batteries—Flak 8.8cm and Pak 40 7.5cm—remained, and it was these more than the panzers that had stopped the British tanks during Operation *Goodwood*. The prospects of a quick breakthrough south were thus slim, and yet this is exactly what General Bernard Montgomery asked of Lieutenant-General Guy Simonds, commander of the Canadian II Corps.

> "Our own tactical methods are thorough and methodical but slow and cumbersome. In consequence, our troops fight well in defence and our set-piece attacks are usually successful, but it is not unfair to say that through lack of enterprise in exploitation, we seldom reap the full benefit of them. We are too flank-conscious, we over-insure administratively, we are by nature too apprehensive of failure and our training makes us more so."
> —Bill McAndrew quoting a British report prior to *Totalize*.

Simonds was not your average general. For him, battle had to be managed scientifically, and using the most original and unusual methods would, he believed, allow him to succeed where others had failed. As the British had already failed a number of times in Normandy, Simonds decided not to make the same mistakes. The best example of "what not to do" was Operation *Goodwood*, where the tanks, after an initial breakthrough facilitated by aerial bombardment, were stopped due to the lack of infantry and artillery support, these not being able to follow the tanks quickly enough.

(Library and Archives Canada)

In Profile:
Lieutenant-General Guy Simonds

Guy Granville Simonds was born to a military family in Ixworth, near Bury St Edmunds, Suffolk, England in 1903, before the family immigrated to Victoria in British Columbia, Canada when Guy was nine. His father, Cecil, was wounded as a colonel on the Western Front in 1918. Before joining the Royal Canadian Horse Artillery as a subaltern in 1926, Simonds won the sword of honor at the Royal Military College of Canada in Kingston, Ontario, an institution he attended from 1921 to 1925.

In the years leading up to the outbreak of war in 1939, Simonds attended various staff and gunnery courses in the UK and Canada. By 1939 Major Simonds was an Associate Professor of Artillery and later an instructor in Tactics at the Royal Military College of Canada. He served with the 1st Canadian Infantry Division in England and then in July 1940 as CO of the 1st Field Regiment, Royal Canadian Artillery, before being promoted to a brigadier under General Harry Crerar until September 1942. By the time of the Sicily landings in 1943, Simonds, the youngest divisional commander in the British Empire at just 40, was a major-general in charge of the 1st Canadian Infantry Division where he caught Montgomery's eye.

In January 1944 he returned to the UK to take command of the Canadian II Corps, and saw continuous action from D-Day, through the Normandy campaign to the liberation of Northwestern Europe, temporarily taking command of the Canadian First Army from his old CO, Harry Crerar. Always something of a hothead, Simonds's career was marred by controversy, something he always managed to rise above; nevertheless, next to Patton, he was probably the most talented Allied general during the Normandy campaign. He died from lung cancer in Toronto in 1974.

In Profile:
Allied Aviation

This P-51D, "Cripes Almighty," belonged to Major George E. Preddy Jr of the 487th Fighter Squadron, 352nd Fighter Group. Preddy had 27 aerial kills and five ground kills to his name. He was hit by American antiaircraft fire on Christmas Day 1944, while chasing a Focke Wulf 190.

Francis S. "Gabby" Gabreski of the 61st Fighter Squadron, 56th Fighter Group, flew this P-47 during the battle of Normandy. He was shot down and taken prisoner on July 20, 1944.

A Hawker Typhoon IB from the 193rd Squadron, 146th Wing. This aircraft was hit near Sourdeval in August 1944, on the westernmost edge of the Falaise Pocket. These aircraft successfully secured dozens of missions in supporting the ground troops.

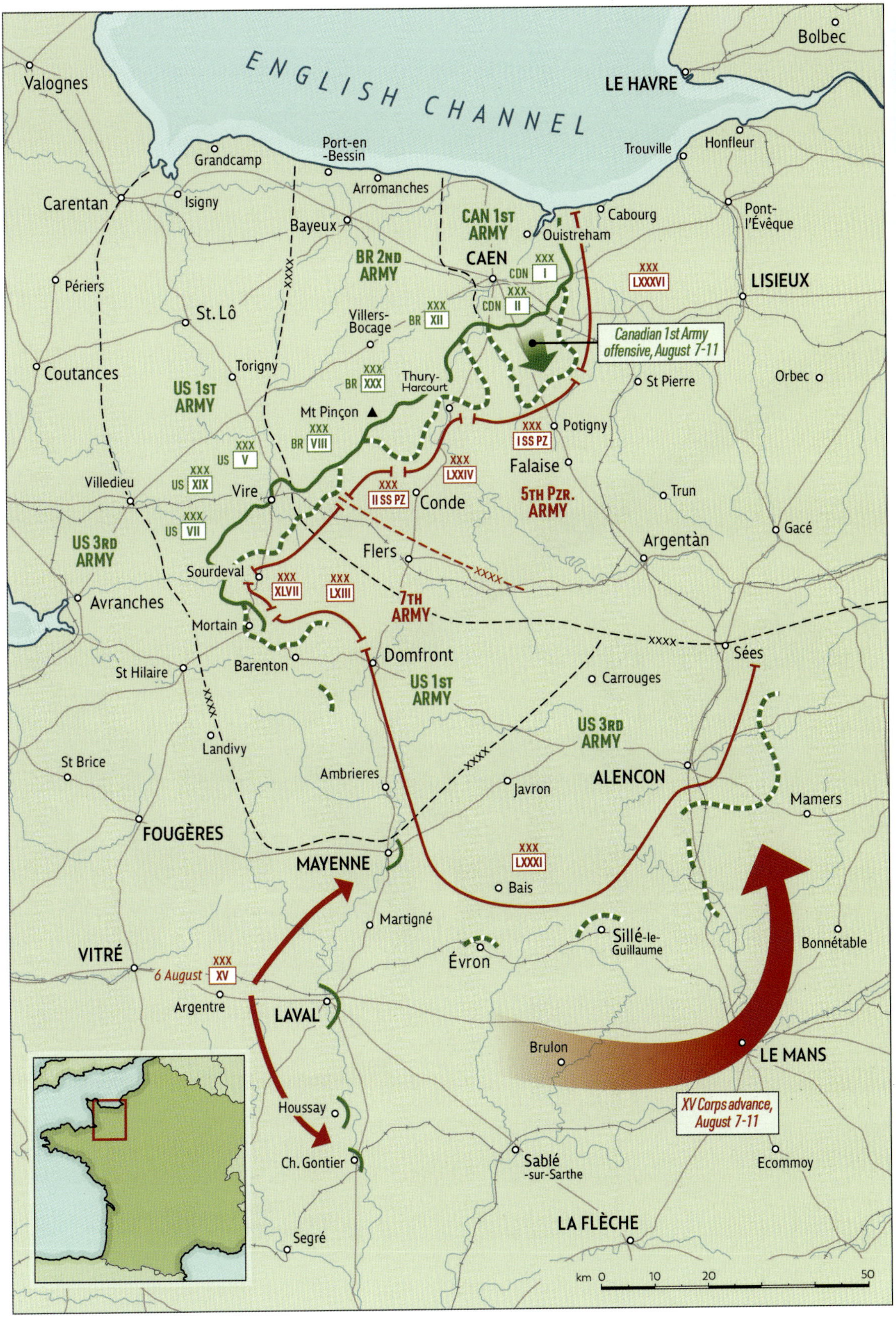
ENGLISH CHANNEL
LE HAVRE
Bolbec
Valognes
Carentan
Grandcamp
Isigny
Port-en-Bessin
Arromanches
Bayeux
Trouville
Honfleur
Cabourg
Ouistreham
Pont-l'Évêque
CAN 1st ARMY
CAEN
BR 2nd ARMY
LISIEUX
LXXXVI
CDN I
CDN II
BR XII
Périers
St. Lô
Villers-Bocage
Canadian 1st Army offensive, August 7-11
Coutances
Torigny
US 1st ARMY
BR XXX
Thury-Harcourt
St Pierre
Orbec
Mt Pinçon
I SS PZ
Potigny
BR VIII
US V
LXXIV
Falaise
US XIX
Villedieu
Vire
II SS PZ
Conde
5th PZR. ARMY
Trun
US VII
US 3rd ARMY
Gacé
Argentàn
Flers
Sourdeval
XLVII
LXIII
Avranches
7th ARMY
Mortain
Domfront
Sées
St Hilaire
Barenton
Carrouges
US 1st ARMY
US 3rd ARMY
Landivy
St Brice
Ambrieres
Javron
ALENCON
Mamers
FOUGÈRES
MAYENNE
LXXXI
Bais
Martigné
Sillé-le-Guillaume
Bonnétable
VITRÉ
6 August
XV
Évron
Argentre
LAVAL
Brulon
LE MANS
Houssay
XV Corps advance, August 7-11
Ch. Gontier
Sablé-sur-Sarthe
Ecommoy
LA FLÈCHE
Segré
km 0 10 20 50

The Pak 8.8cm cannon was as formidable, if not more so, than the more common Flak 8.8cm, as it was shorter and therefore easier to maneuver. This example was destroyed on August 8, 1944, during Operation *Totalize*. (IWM B8832)

Operation *Totalize* posed two challenges for Simonds: first, he had to find a means of getting all his tanks and infantry to the German positions at the same time, so they might attack the second line before the defenders had a chance to regroup, and second, he had to be able to provide enough fire support for the armored divisions to allow them to begin their operations without having to wait for the arrival of the artillery.

The solution Simonds came up with, which would also introduce the element of surprise to the assault, was to attack at night, without any artillery preparation. He would strike between the principal points of German resistance with compact tank columns, accompanied by infantry in armored vehicles—these including, for the lack of anything better, a number of M7 self-propelled artillery pieces stripped of their 105mm guns. The plan was to have the infantry dismount from the vehicles once they reached a point 5 kilometers inside the German lines, so as to attack the second line on foot.

Simonds decided to utilize heavy bombers as support in two phases: Bomber Command would attack during the night, overwhelming the German defenses on both sides of the attack corridor, then the medium and heavy American bombers would provide support from the afternoon of the next day.

As the attack would be taking place at night, which was not a tactic often used by the British, several precautions were taken to ensure the tanks and the infantry did not lose their way in the dark. For example, the lead tanks were to be directed by a radio-goniometric

The 9th SS Panzer Division Hohenstaufen on the road. The division had just left the sector south of Caen when the Canadians attacked. (ECPAD)

A Sherman from 3 Troop, 1st Northants Yeomanry at Cormelles. The regiment is supporting the 1st Black Watch, an infantry battalion of the 51st Highland Division. (IWM B8796)

system—to obtain the bearing in radio direction finding, or RDF—and to avoid mistakes on the flanks, antiaircraft Bofors guns would fire tracer shells, while spotlights would enhance the natural moonlight.

Another Black August 8 for the German Army?

On August 8, 1918, the Allied offensive on the Somme had marked the beginning of the end for the German Army. After the conflict, that day was declared by Erich Ludendorff "the black day of the German Army."

Twenty-six years later, Canadian General Henry Crerar noted that, at a general staff meeting just before Operation *Totalize* commenced, all the officers present were in a state of great euphoria, so pleased were they with Lieutenant-General Simonds's plan. As quoted from his diary under "Remarks to senior officers," Simonds himself reportedly said: "I have no doubt that we shall make the 8th of August 1944 an even blacker day for the German Armies than is recorded against that same date twenty-six years ago." He even believed that a Canadian victory would be the catalyst for the collapse of the German presence in Normandy and a quick end to the war.

The 7th Armoured Division supported the Durhams to good effect in the sector south of Mont Pinçon, though this front was relatively quiet during Operation *Totalize*. (IWM B6887)

In Profile:
German Tanks

A Panzer IV H from the 6/2nd SS Panzer Division Das Reich. The Das Reich played an important role in the breakout by attacking the Polish from outside the Falaise Pocket before it closed.

A Tiger from the 2nd Company, 101st SS Heavy Panzer Battalion commanded by Uscha Warmbrunn. The two heavy Waffen-SS battalions helped delay the Canadians en route to Falaise.

A Panther G belonging to the 2nd Battalion, 33rd Panzer Regiment.

On the evening of August 7, the two assault divisions assembled south of Caen, in six long and straight columns composed of flail tanks (to detonate any mines), conventional tanks, infantry vehicles and self-propelled guns. The tanks advanced four abreast.

To the west of the Caen–Falaise road and in the general direction of Bretteville-sur-Laize, the assault would be led by Canadian units, specifically the 4th Infantry Brigade and the 2nd Armoured Brigade. To the east of the road and toward the Cramesnil, Saint-Aignan sector, it would be two British units, the 154th Infantry Brigade (51st Division) and the 33rd Armoured Brigade.

At 2300 hours, the Royal Air Force (RAF) bombardment began, and half an hour later the columns set off, following a creeping artillery barrage. The plan did not go quite as well as was hoped, as the dust from the vehicles and the bombs, combined with a smokescreen thrown up by the Germans, brought visibility down to almost zero. This caused some confusion resulting in collisions, loss of bearings, and uncontrolled gunfire. Several armored vehicles were hit—perhaps by German, perhaps by friendly fire—with the burning hulks proving convenient markers for the German artillery. But for the most part, the columns moved in the right direction, and while the poor visibility caused confusion for the Allies, it was as equally bad for the Germans.

To the east of the Orne, an artillery column heads for the front. The 25-pounder saw heavy use in Normandy, supporting the tank attacks. During Operation *Totalize* the Canadian and Polish armored divisions had to make do without these guns. (IWM B9166)

The experience of one of the columns advancing to the east of the Caen–Falaise road is perhaps representative. Very quickly, the three tanks leading the column with navigational aids fell into massive bomb craters and could not get out. In an attempt to avoid them, and the same fate, the others following lost all cohesion.

This Sherman armored recovery vehicle (ARV) is a Mark III with its turret removed, repurposed for the recovery and repair of British armored vehicles in the field. This vehicle probably belonged to one of the ten light workshops of the Royal Electrical and Mechanical Engineers (REME), 79th Armoured Division, judging by the insignia—an inverted triangle and bull's head—painted at the front of the tank. (IWM B8990)

A Panzer IV H, with luxuriant camouflage, from the 12th SS Panzer Division Hitlerjugend—the unit that stopped the Canadian offensive on the Falaise road. (ECPAD)

In Profile:
American Artillery and Tanks

An American M12 155mm self-propelled gun. Following Bradley's decision to halt the Third Army south of Argentan, American artillery was deployed in the sector to batter the roads and logistical infrastructure still held by the Germans in Trun-Chambois.

An American 105mm howitzer that pounded German positions in the Argentan sector. The town was almost completely razed before being taken by the Americans.

An M4 Sherman from the 5th Armored Division. This unit played an important role in the formation of the Falaise Pocket, then in the advance on Paris.

An SdKfz 250 of the 12th SS Panzer Division Hitlerjugend. (ECPAD)

Changing the engine of a light Stuart, near Caumont. The tank belongs to the British 8th Armoured Brigade. (IWM B8891)

A Flakvierling from the 12th SS Panzer Division Hitlerjugend. In defensive positions, well camouflaged, the German units held their own against superior Allied aviation, but they could only move at night. (ECPAD)

The same task—changing an engine—in the same place, but with an M4-A1 Sherman. The new engine is a Continental, derived from an aircraft model. (IWM B8892)

Lieutenant-Colonel Jolly, Commanding Officer (CO) of the 144th Regiment, Royal Armoured Corps, described the scene as one of indescribable chaos; each tank had instructions to follow the tank in front of his own but that it soon became apparent it was a case of the blind leading the blind.

To restore order, the officers dismounted from the tanks and armored vehicles and Jolly himself, on foot, fired flares to mark the way. Thus, the advance was resumed and despite the delay, the infantry progressed a further 200 meters from their latest jump-off position and were in easy reach of their objective, Cramesnil, with just a dozen fatalities.

By daybreak, the British columns had reached their objectives and were solidly established 5 kilometers inside the German lines. The Canadians had progressed just as far, but German resistance had been more ferocious in their sector and not all their objectives had been achieved, but by afternoon all but one had fallen. The first phase of the offensive had succeeded, and everything seemed to indicate that it would rapidly transform into a new, decisive breakthrough.

When one thinks of German armor in the battle of Normandy one immediately thinks of the panzer divisions, while other armored units have been all but forgotten, notably those of the Sturmgeschütz, the self-propelled guns. This vehicle belongs to the 302nd Panzer Battalion Fkl (Funklenk), which had 40 StuG IIIs as well as BIV (the Borgward IV) remote-controlled exploding tanks. The unit was created in October 1942 at Neuruppin from the remnants of 3rd Battalion, 10th Panzer Regiment. (ECPAD)

One of the 302nd Panzer Battalion's Borgward IVs. The Borgward IV, the largest German remote-controlled demolition vehicle in use during the war, and unlike the smaller Springer and Goliath, was driven by an operator who would then evacuate the BIV and control its advance to its target by radio. (ECPAD)

The German Reaction

During the evening of August 8, von Kluge made several telephone calls. He told Waffen-SS General Paul Hausser: "A breakthrough, the likes of which we have never seen, is now taking place at Caen."

A little later, he spoke with one of his panzer commanders, General Hans Eberbach: "We didn't think it would come so quickly, but I imagine that it doesn't surprise you."

Eberbach responded: "No, I've been waiting for this. Every day I thought it would be the next."

On the ground, command fell to General Kurt Meyer, commander of the 12th SS Panzer Division Hitlerjugend. When the Bomber Command raid stopped, Meyer took the road from Caen to Falaise, where he found scattered groups of soldiers in complete disarray. He gathered them together without much difficulty and placed them in defensive positions on the heights of Cintheaux. This done, he reinforced the infantry with antitank pieces and a few armored vehicles and, most importantly, he sent his two *kampfgruppen* ahead to immediately counterattack north of Cintheaux.

This was a wise decision, though Meyer didn't see it that way when his counterattack failed. However, it saved his tanks, which bypassed Cintheaux to the north as the U.S. Eighth Air Force bombers materialized and flattened the suburbs of Cintheaux and Bretteville-sur-Laize.

Senior German POWs at Trent Park Camp, London, in November 1944. Standing from left: Generalleutnant Otto Elfeldt (Heer, captured in the Falaise Pocket), Generalleutnant Ferdinand Heim (Heer) and Generalmajor Gerhard Bassenge (Heer); seated from left: Generalleutnant Fritz Broich (Heer), General der Panzertruppe Heinrich Eberbach (Heer), Generalmajor Georg Neuffer (Luftwaffe) and Oberst Hans Reimann (Heer). (Bundesarchiv, MSg 2 Bild-14835-08 / Unknown / CC-BY-SA 3.0)

In Profile:
General Hans Eberbach

Heinrich "Hans" Eberbach was born in 1895 in Stuttgart. In July 1914, he signed on with the Army of Württemberg, seeing significant action on the Western Front during the first year of the war. He was wounded by shrapnel in the thigh on October 16, 1914, and was then captured by French troops in September 1915, being severely wounded in the face: he lost his nose. After his release in 1919, he became a policeman, until the formation of the Wehrmacht in 1935, and took part in the invasion of Poland as commander of a panzer regiment in the 4th Panzer Division under Major-General Georg-Hans Reinhardt.

He participated in the invasion of France, crossing the Meuse with General Manteuffel's offensive. In June 1941, with Operation *Barbarossa*, he found himself as commander of the 5th Panzer Brigade in Geyr von Schweppenburg's XXIV Panzer Corps. It was during the battle of Moscow that Eberbach demonstrated his superior military prowess, by breaking through the Soviet front, advancing some 120 kilometers and almost destroying the Soviet Bryansk Front. In March 1942, he assumed command of the 4th Panzer Division, and six months later the XLVIII Panzer Corps. He was wounded at Stalingrad and repatriated.

Appointed *General der Panzertruppe* during the Normandy invasion, he took command of Panzer Group West (5th Panzer Army). A superb strategist, he appreciated the Germans stood little chance in the Normandy campaign, proposing a wholesale withdrawal to the Seine. He led the counteroffensive at Mortain—he predicted that it was doomed—before being given command of the remnants of the 7th Army in the Falaise Pocket. He escaped but was captured by British troops shortly thereafter on August 31, at Amiens. He died in 1992, aged ninety-six.

In Profile: German Aviation

The Focke-Wulf 190 A4 of Oberleutnant Joseph Wurmhaller, from the 26th Fighter Wing, or more correctly, the 9. Staffel/Jagdgeschwader 26 (9/JG 26), shot down on June 22, 1944 after recording 102 kills. The aircraft shown here dates from August/September 1943, a year before its demise, when it had 77 kills to its name.

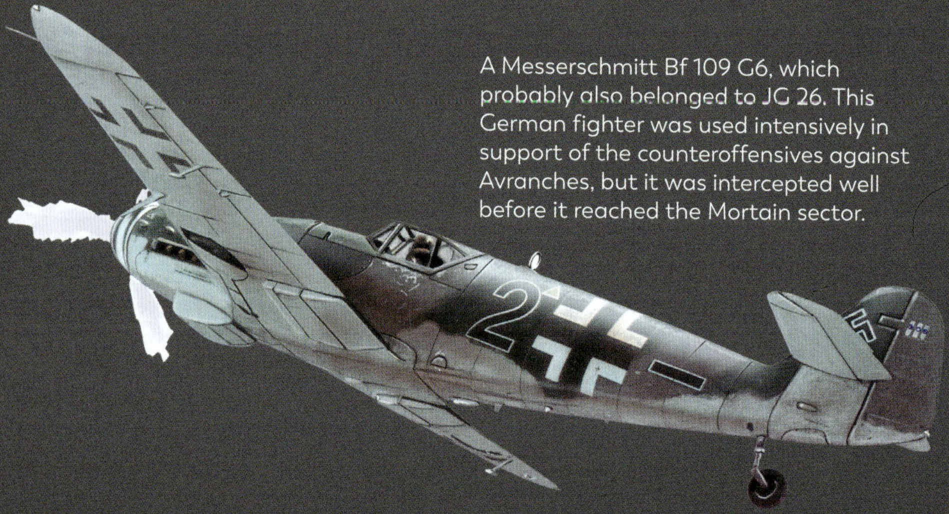

A Messerschmitt Bf 109 G6, which probably also belonged to JG 26. This German fighter was used intensively in support of the counteroffensives against Avranches, but it was intercepted well before it reached the Mortain sector.

A Junkers 88 G1 from NJG 2 (2nd Night Fighter Wing). German night fighters were used over Normandy to escort the Heinkel 111s ferrying supplies into the Falaise Pocket; the roads could no longer be used as they were dedicated to the retreat to the Seine.

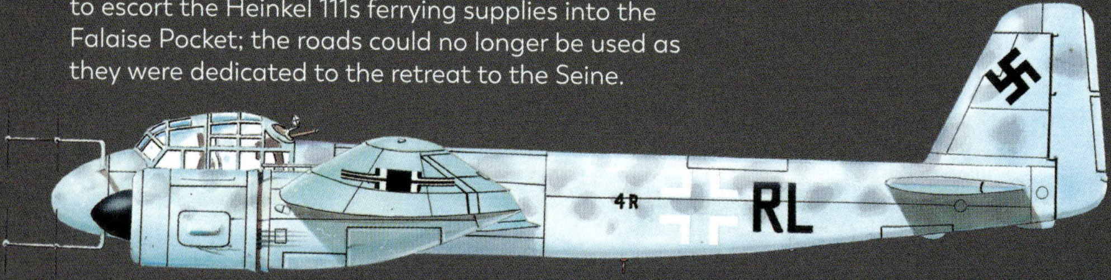

Around midday, two Allied armored divisions—the 4th Canadian and the 1st Polish—were preparing to advance on Falaise and exploit the breakthrough of the previous day.

The Poles were stopped in their tracks mid-afternoon by the 12th SS Panzer Division Hitlerjugend. On the other side of the road, the Germans held Cintheaux until that evening, thus preventing the Canadians from exploiting the previous night's breakthrough. This double failure was due in part to the fact that these two divisions had not seen combat and therefore lacked experience. Instead of asking for the support of their artillery or Allied fighter-bombers, they fought on alone and, worse, tried to reduce all the nodes of German resistance they encountered instead of driving forward and leaving them to be mopped up later, as Simonds had ordered.

It would be wrong to blame the Poles for not being able to force their way through, as they were up against the battle-hardened 12th SS Panzer Division Hitlerjugend. However, the Canadians should have done better in the face of much weaker opposition.

By nightfall, the two Allied divisions, instead of continuing their efforts, went on the defensive, giving the Germans time to regroup. They had missed their opportunity, and failed to progress 5 kilometers that day.

During the night, Simonds sent a mixed armored column to assault Hill 195 in the hope of regaining the element of surprise he had enjoyed the previous day, but this time the attack fared badly. The objective was some distance off, halfway between Cintheaux and Falaise, and the column got lost in the dark, and fell into the sights of a battery of 8.8cm guns, which caused mayhem and significant casualties. The Waffen-SS counterattacked throughout the following day, and while the Canadians managed to stand their ground, they were forced to abandon their positions at nightfall, having lost no fewer than 45 tanks.

On August 9, the Germans fell back to the Laison, which finally allowed the Canadians to conquer Hill 195, coming to within a dozen kilometers of Falaise. *Totalize* was not a resounding success and no significant breakthrough had been accomplished. It was evident that a renewed effort on the part of Montgomery was needed to seize Falaise.

On the German side, the masterly way in which the Canadian operation had been halted renewed von Kluge's confidence. On the morning of August 9, he told a staff officer, Major-General Rudolf Freiherr von Gersdorff: "I have just had a very important conference with the OKW. The situation south of Caen having been re-established and not having had the consequences we feared, I propose we revisit the idea of a counteroffensive [on Mortain]. But at present, the operation would have to be especially well prepared and unhurried."

A New German Plan

The new German plan was mostly the work of Hitler himself. He openly reproached von Kluge for having attacked too soon: "He did it intentionally to show that my orders could not be executed." This time, command was entrusted to Eberbach, who handed his command of the 5th Panzer Army to Paul Hausser.

A 302nd Panzer Battalion StuG III. Note the tactical symbol on the mudguard, a small number 4, meaning this vehicle belonged to the 4th Company.

An SdKfz 251 D of the 9th SS Panzer Division Hohenstaufen. (ECPAD)

Eberbach accepted that his new mission could barely be more than defensive in nature, especially as he had to improvise a staff. He chose the best officers that he had at his disposal, notably Lieutenant-Colonel von Kluge, son of the field marshal and Arthur von Eckesparre, formerly of Field Marshal Erwin Rommel's staff, as the makeshift army corps prepared for the counteroffensive.

The 116th Panzer Division was withdrawn from the front in view of its participation in the attack, the XLVII Panzer Corps followed suit as did the 1st SS Panzer Division LSSAH. These units would form the spearhead of the offensive. Behind them would come the Panther battalion of the 9th Panzer Division and two Nebelwerfer brigades. The attack was to be launched from the Mortain–Domfront region, first toward Saint-Hilaire, then on to Avranches.

In his calculations, Eberbach realized that it would be impossible for him to attack on August 11 as planned. Firstly, he could only assemble 77 Panzer IVs and 47 Panthers, which he judged insufficient. He also needed replacement vehicles, spares, extra ordnance and munitions, but most importantly, he needed time. Due to the superiority of the Allied air effort, he could only attack before dawn, in the small hours, when the fog was still low. At best, he thought, he could fight between 0400 and 1000 hours. If the troops did not reach their objectives within this time period, they would be discovered by the Allied fighter-bombers, as at Mortain.

For an effective nighttime attack, launching just after nightfall, Eberbach would have to wait for the full moon, which was not due to appear until August 20. As this date corresponded with a forecasted decline in weather conditions, which would hamper the Allied aircraft, Eberbach asked to postpone the attack until that date. He needed Hitler's permission, which was not an easy thing to secure, and in the meantime a series of significant events was about to threaten all the German plans.

The Franco-American Envelopment

On the evening of August 10, 1944, von Kluge received some worrying news: the U.S. XV Corps had veered away from its path to Le Mans and was now on its way to Alençon. The Americans were trying to surround the German 7th Army. And von Kluge had nothing in that region with which to oppose them.

This photograph is often mistakenly identified as having been taken in the Falaise Pocket, near Trun or Chambois, but was in fact taken by the Americans in the Sourdeval sector, near Mortain. The matériel in the bottom right-hand corner, including an SdKfz 251 D and a Schwimmwagen, is from an armored SS division. The pressure applied by the Americans in the Sourdeval sector forced the Germans to engage the 10th SS Panzer Division Frundsberg, so it is probable that these abandoned vehicles belong to this formation. (DITE/USIS)

Two German reconnaissance vehicles scuttled by their crews are burning at the edge of a wood. An American armored column has stopped to have a look. (DITE/USIS)

German prisoners of war, mostly Luftwaffe, captured at Chateaudun are being escorted by a lone GI. (DITE/USIS)

For the commander in chief of the German forces, the one and only solution was to abandon the counteroffensive on Mortain and return with the panzer divisions to face the Americans threatening Alençon. The town was key for the Germans, as it served as a rear base for the 7th Army, and was therefore a crucial source for munitions, fuel, supplies, and other necessities.

The term G.I.—originally "galvanized iron"—to describe an American soldier (and airman) came about during World War I, with U.S. troops referring to incoming German artillery shells as "G.I. cans." In 1918, the initialism morphed into "government issue" or "general issue" to describe any item of military issue, including soldiers. The term came into common usage during the draft of 1940.

On the evening of August 10, von Kluge called Jodl to convince Hitler to give orders to this effect. For once, the Führer did not refuse outright; however, in his opinion, the fight against the U.S. XV Corps would have to wait until a decisive counteroffensive at Mortain was completed. In other words, Hitler's approval was not forthcoming. Von Kluge called back several times on the morning of August 11.

The situation on the ground deteriorated quickly, with the 9th Panzer Division already forced back to Alençon by the superior American forces. Von Kluge sent an urgent memorandum to Hitler, in which he implored the Führer to authorize an attack on the U.S. XV Corps on August 14, with the 1st SS Panzer Division and the 2nd and 116th Panzer Divisions. Hitler agreed, but wanted to widen the scope of the attack, with a view to ultimately reconquering the entire sector as far as Le Mans. At the same time, he authorized a marginal withdrawal in the Sourdeval–Mortain sector, which began during the night of August 11/12, as Eberbach prepared to stop the American advance on Alençon.

An American infantry column marches on in the area of Saint-Saveur de Chaulieu. The GI on the right is carrying a Browning M1917A1 heavy machine gun on his shoulder. (DITE/USIS)

An antiaircraft battery near Saint-Hilaire du Harcouet. This is a 40mm Bofors cannon. German aviation did not pose much of a threat, especially during the day. (DITE/USIS)

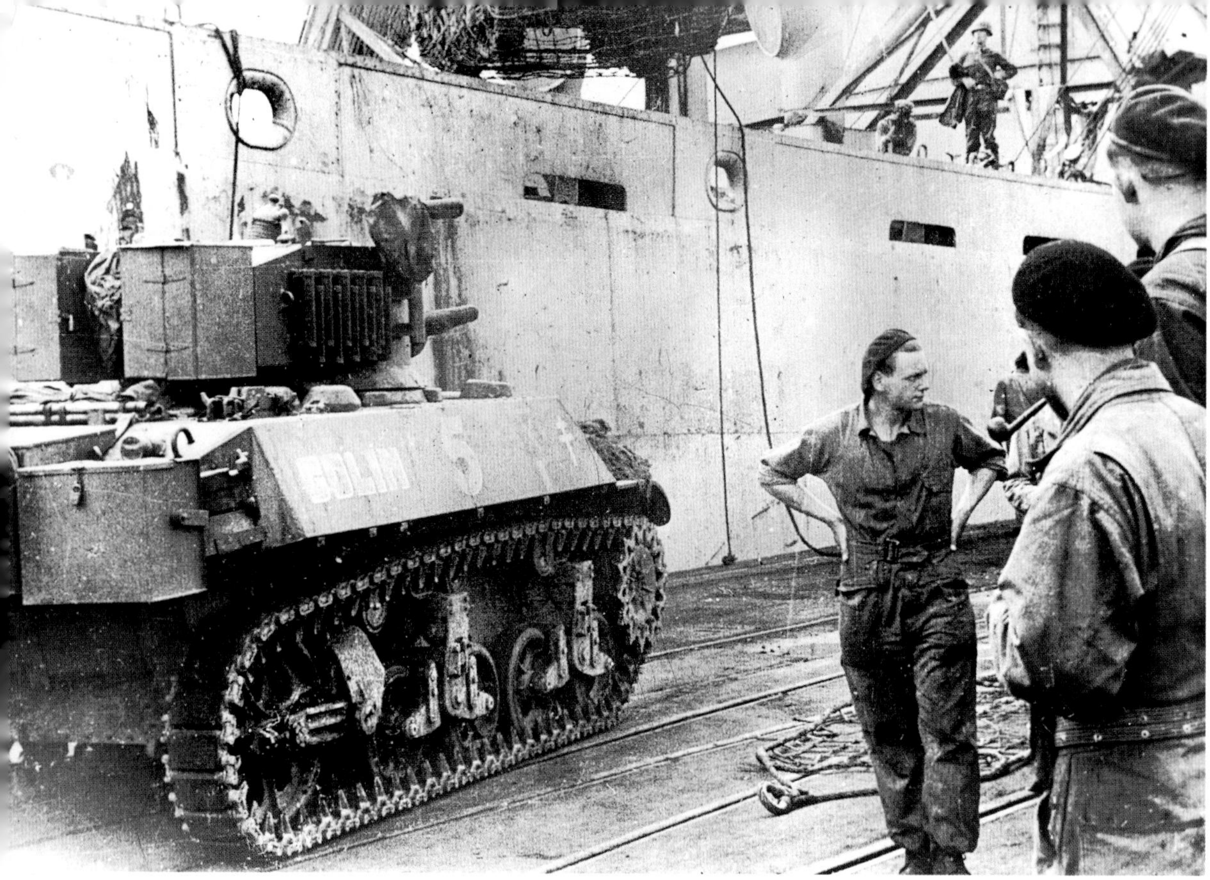

A French 2nd Armored Division Stuart tank just before departing England. The straight-sided rear of the hull shows that this is an M3A3 rather than an M5. (ECPAD)

The French 2nd Armored Division boarding an LST (Landing Ship, Tank). Its large doors were located at the stern only, so vehicles had to enter the hold in reverse gear, with of course the exception of motorcycles. (ECPAD)

A column of French Shermans passes through an English seaside resort before boarding the LSTs that will transport them to Normandy in early August. (ECPAD)

FFIs (French Forces of the Interior) also participated in the battle of Normandy, notably thanks to their local knowledge and information. (IWM B9369)

The French 2nd Armored Division's landing at Utah Beach did not go unnoticed. Here, General Walker warmly welcomes General Leclerc de Hautecloque. (ECPAD)

The American Plan

The idea of a rapid envelopment of the Germans was suggested for the first time on August 8 by General Omar Bradley, while Eisenhower was visiting his headquarters. The Americans, he suggested, should execute a 90-degree change in direction, veering northward. The First Army would then move from the Barenton–Domfront sector to Flers, while the Third Army took Alençon then advanced toward Argentan, where it would meet the Canadian II Corps, effectively surrounding the bulk of the German troops.

On August 11, Montgomery suggested a similar maneuver, though he believed that the Germans would do everything possible to stop the Americans from seizing Alençon. Because of this, he advised that Argentan should be taken by the Canadians, via Falaise, rather than by the Americans. This would turn out to be a fateful recommendation.

The 2nd French Armored Division Joins the Fray

General Wade H. Haislip's U.S. XV Corps took Le Mans on August 8 with the 5th Armored Division and the 79th and 90th Infantry Divisions. It was here that he received orders to advance on Alençon. To give him a larger offensive force, Patton assigned Haislip the French 2nd Armored Division of General Leclerc de Hautecloque, which landed at Utah Beach at the beginning of August.

The French 2nd Armored Division was divided into four GTs, or GT (*groupes tactiques,* i.e. Combat Commands): GT Dio, which included the 12th Cuirassiers; GT Billotte, with the 501st Tank Regiment; GT Rémy, including the 1st Moroccan Spahi Regiment; and finally GT Langlade, with the 12th African Chasseurs. Each tactical group also contained infantry and artillery units. Altogether, these amounted to an impressive total of 4,000 vehicles, which began to arrive at Le Mans on August 9.

Cuirassiers originated in the late 15th-century Europe. Evolving from medieval men-at-arms and demi-lancers swapping their lances for pistols, cuirassiers were heavy cavalry, not dissimilar to the English dragoons, although the English themselves utilized cuirassier regiments. The term originates from the *cuirasse*, the heavy armored breastplate—and later backplate—that was worn. The cuirassiers saw their finest hours during the Napoleonic wars, but continued as mounted cavalry well into the late 19th century, with even a few units still in action during World War I. By the advent of World War II, all cavalry units—cuirassiers, dragoons, hussars and the like—had evolved into armored cavalry units, i.e. tanks.

The German Situation

The Germans did not have sufficient troops to oppose the U.S. XV Corps, and had to wait for the arrival of Eberbach's panzer divisions. What they did have was the 708th Infantry Division, though this unit was not considered to be high quality, and the 9th Panzer Division, whose Panther battalion was being held at Falaise. A *kampfgruppe* of paratroopers from the 6th Fallschirmjäger Division was expected, but did not arrive before the battle began. The remains of the Panzer Lehr Division and the 352nd Infantry Division, once powerful but now severely depleted, were left to hold the second line.

The media coverage of the French 2nd Armored Division's landing continues. As Leclerc and his aides leave Utah Beach, a photographer changes the plate in his camera. (ECPAD)

Sergeant Charles H. Coolidge, from Signal Mountain, Tenn., a member of Company M, 141st Infantry Regiment, 36th Infantry Division, VI Corps, is congratulated by General Wade H. Haislip, CG U.S. Seventh Army, after being presented with the Congressional Medal of Honor, for meritorious service in leading a section of heavy machine gunners who took and held a position east of Belmont-sur-Buttant, France, on October 24, 1944, until it was apparent that the position could no longer be defended. (National Archives and Records Administration, NAID 440)

In Profile:
General Wade H. Haislip

Nicknamed "Ham," Wade Hampton Haislip was born in Woodstock, Virginia in 1889. He graduated West Point in 1912 and was commissioned a second lieutenant in the infantry, serving in Vera Cruz, Mexico in 1914. He joined the American Expeditionary Forces and was transferred to the Western Front in 1917, where he took part in the battle of Saint-Mihiel and the Meuse-Argonne Offensive. He served on the General Staff, U.S. Forces in Germany until 1921 before returning to West Point as an instructor until 1923.

Between the wars he attended various military colleges—the U.S. Army Infantry School, the Command and General Staff School, the Ecole supérieure de guerre in Paris, and the U.S. Army War College—before assignments with the War Department General Staff. In World War II he served as commander of the 85th Infantry Division before taking over command of XV Corps from March 1943 until the end of the war in Europe, where he saw action in campaigns in Normandy, France, the Rhineland, and Central Europe. He then became commander of the U.S. Seventh Army until August 1945. He retired in 1951, becoming Governor of the Soldiers' Home in Washington, D.C. He died following a stroke in 1971. Haislip was a personal friend of Eisenhower's, and in fact introduced Mamie Dowd to him when they were serving together as lieutenants, Dwight a junior one, at Fort Sam Houston.

Near the British XII Corps general headquarters, *maquisards* take up positions on a truck that they have just captured and repainted with the cross of Lorraine. It is easy to imagine that British officers were unimpressed by these fighters in their un-military clothing and makeshift vehicles. (IWM B9420)

On August 11, in spite the slow advance of the two Allied armored divisions, the French 2nd Armored Division still managed to get within 5 kilometers of Alençon. The 9th Panzer Division and the 352nd Infantry Division destroyed 36 Allied tanks, which is not insignificant, but the state of the panzer division at this point was alarming, as Eberbach himself noted when he came to assess the situation at Alençon. He estimated his forces at one infantry battalion, one artillery battalion, and a dozen Panzer IVs. Eberbach planned to bring in the 116th Panzer Division over the next few hours, but in waiting for it to arrive, he put Argentan into a state of siege, knowing that Alençon could not be held.

The 12th Cuirassiers Take Alençon

Captain Gaudet and his 4th Squadron, 12th Cuirassiers had been sent on a reconnaissance mission by General Leclerc. Progressing quickly, Gaudet was certain that there was no longer any enemy presence ahead of them, but as night fell, he stopped: "I decided to stop because I was sure that there would be nothing ahead. And also because it was becoming difficult to see anything. I formed a plan that was neither coherent nor organized: defense to the north, protection to the right, protection to the left … I was dog-tired! Ready to drop!"

Chasseurs, from the French word for "hunter," are essentially light infantry (*chasseurs à pied*) and light cavalry (*chasseurs à cheval*), utilized principally in French and Belgian forces. Originating during the War of the Austrian Succession in 1743, chasseurs have remained a distinct branch of the French army, with the rapid-reaction component being their primary modus operandus. Today the French army boasts several permutations of the chasseurs: alpine (mountain troops), paratrooper, armor, mechanized infantry, and light infantry.

An iconic depiction of American tactics following the breakthrough at Avranches: in the case of resolute German opposition, the tanks would call on the fighter-bombers to attack the enemy. Here, the crew of a heavily laden.M5 Stuart observe the effects of a P-47 Thunderbolt strike. (DITE/USIS)

By this time, Leclerc was also asleep, in the open, but at around 0200 hours, a German mortar shell hit the stationary half-track full force, killing two subalterns and starting a blaze. Leclerc awoke and left immediately in search of Gaudet to find out where the reconnaissance force had got to. The captain was woken with a start by his batman, Aït Abbat, who declared, "Sir! … the general … he's here!'

At 0300 hours, the squadron was back on the road to Alençon, accompanied by tank destroyers, self-propelled artillery and half-tracks. Lieutenant Mucchieli's recollection of the journey is particularly evocative:

> An endless column on the road. We see nothing. No gunshots. We hear nothing but the sound of idling engines. No screams. The squadron is somewhere in this slow march, in the smoke that thickens the night. Houses, streets, houses again. We are in Alençon. A pale day begins to break, and locals begin to leave their houses. It's daytime. Cries from below drift up to us. Groups of men and women shout *"Vive les Americains!"* ["Long live the Americans!"] When we respond in French, they shout, *"Ce sont des Canadiens!"* ["They're Canadian!"] When we display our Lorraine crosses on our tanks and chests, the news runs through the town and the people are full of joyful tears. A patrol from the 2nd platoon goes to reconnoiter a barricade and is welcomed with shots of Calvados.

Armed with American M1 carbines, *maquisards* talk to British soldiers at XII Corps GHQ.

American artillery fires on German positions in the Argentan sector. This is a 155mm howitzer at full recoil. (DITE/USIS)

The rear of a German motorized column near Saint-Aubin d'Appenais in August 1944. The remains of at least two SdKfz 251s can be seen. The registration plate of the vehicle on the left shows that it is a Heer, not a Waffen-SS vehicle. (ECPAD)

This SdKfz 251 has taken a direct hit, which has pierced its armor plate and started a fire. The matériel losses suffered by the Germans in August 1944 were considerable, but the Allied tendency to refer to all and any vehicles as "armored" led to improbably high, and potentially misleading, success rates. (DITE/USIS)

August 12, Alençon

As the French were entering Alençon, the 5th Armored Division was doing the same at Sées, giving the undeniable impression that the Argentan road was open. But the French and Americans were about to trip over each other. Tasked with taking Carrouges and then Ecouché, Leclerc found himself facing the Ecouves forest, a vast wooded massif. Haislip had ordered the French to circumvent the forest to the west, but Leclerc, to avoid unwelcome surprises, decided to send out three tactical groups in advance: one to the west, as planned, another straight through the center of the forest, and another to the east, taking a road reserved for the Americans. Haislip then complained that this breach of orders on the part of the French delayed their attack on Argentan by six hours. In war, neighboring units are often accused of being the cause of each other's setbacks. While it is impossible to determine that the French caused the delay, what is certain is that it gave the Germans the extra six hours they needed to save Argentan. In effect, the 116th Panzer Division began to regroup in the sector as one of its *kampfgruppen* arrived just in time to stop one of the 5th Armored Division's Combat Commands at Mortée. This saved one of the Germans' crucial supply routes into what was then called the Falaise salient. The situation was more critical than ever, but the Germans were not as yet desperate, as on August 13, the 1st SS Panzer Division and the 2nd Panzer Division were due to arrive in the sector.

The term *maquis* originates from the Corsican word for "bush" or "scrubland," similar to the kind of terrain in southern France, where French resistance fighters would seek refuge and plan their guerrilla activities. They came to be known as *maquisards* or *réseaux de résistance* (lit. "resistance networks") with a group taking its name from its area of operation, e.g. Maquis du Limousin.

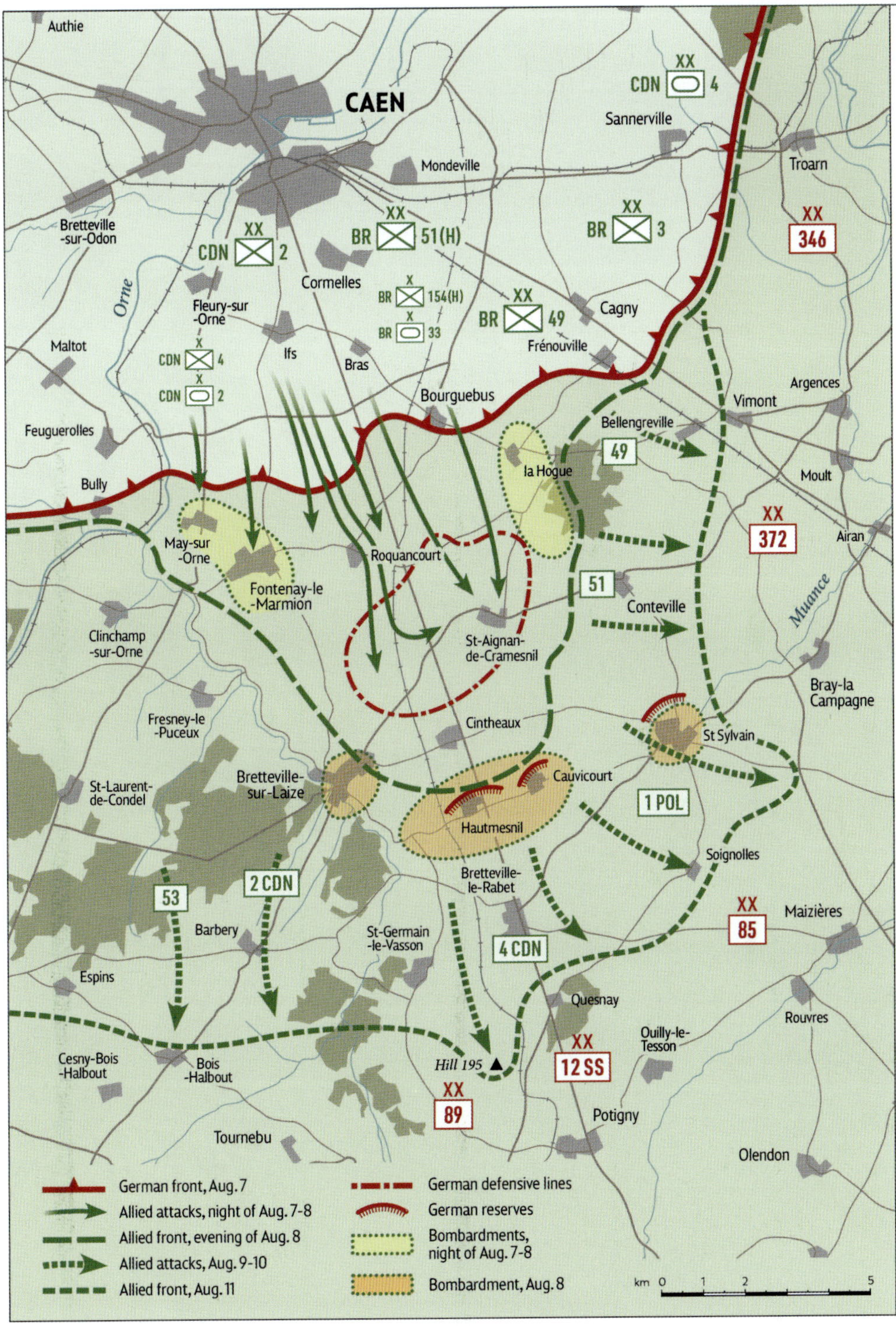

The Western Front August 7–11, 1944, as the Americans changed strategy and abandoned their idea of a rapid advance to the east in favor of surrounding the German armies in Normandy. The U.S. VII Corps would become the linchpin in this change of strategy: abandoning the march on Chartres, it veered off north to Alençon, which served as a rear base and massive depot for the German 7th Army. Following the capture of the town, Hausser's army was deprived of all supplies and had to survive on those of the 5th Panzer Army. The British and Americans then scheduled to link up in the Alençon sector.

These young panzergrenadiers of the 9th SS Panzer Division Hohenstaufen still manage a smile. They considered themselves the most seasoned soldiers of the war and superior to their Allied counterparts, but events that followed soon taught them not to underestimate their adversaries. (ECPAD)

The Allies Delude Themselves

While Eberbach was in the process of consolidating a defensive front (from which he hoped to be able to counterattack in any direction), the two Allied armored divisions were sending unrealistic reports. They announced the capture of 1,500 German prisoners, which is very possible, but also the destruction of 100 panzers, which was, at this time, wildly ambitious, as only the 116th Panzer Division had yet arrived in the sector, and in Eberbach's estimation, they had only a dozen or so tanks. It is possible that the French discovered a number of damaged or half-repaired tanks in Alençon and used them to pad out the numbers, but even so, 100 tanks seems more than a slight exaggeration.

Eberbach, however, was suffering no illusions. He knew that if the Canadians reached Falaise and the Americans reached Argentan, a corridor of only around 20 kilometers would remain through which the Germans might conduct a retreat. This would be disaster without precedent on the Western Front.

Eberbach also tried to establish, as best he could, a left flank. To accomplish this, he had at his disposal the remainder of the 352nd Infantry Division, the 331st Infantry Division (which was just arriving in the sector), and a strong *kampfgruppe* of paratroopers from the

General Bradley interrogates a member of the Waffen-SS. Behind him, to the left, a Heer officer wears a peaked cap that predates the war. Bradley's decision to halt the Third Army before Falaise allowed a large proportion of the German troops that would have been caught in the Falaise Pocket to escape. (DITE/USIS)

6th Fallschirmjäger Division. This was not much to hold a front of some 150 kilometers in length, but it was the best he could do.

The Americans at Falaise

Realizing that he could quickly reach Argentan with the French 2nd Armored Division, Haislip requested Patton's authorization to launch the 5th Armored Division toward Falaise, in contradiction of Montgomery's orders.

Very early on August 13, Patton gave his consent for a "slow" advance on Falaise, even though the Canadians had yet to arrive in-theater. The same day, Leclerc finished clearing the Ecouves forest, where he destroyed most of what remained of the 9th Panzer Division. One patrol even reached Argentan, though it was quickly chased away by panzers.

All other Allied attempts in that direction failed, with large numbers of tanks succumbing to artillery fire and the panzers of the 116th Panzer Division, well hidden among the heights of Argentan. The front was holding, and Bradley was about to issue a controversial order.

A Jagdpanther of the 654th Heavy Panzerjäger (tank-destroyer) Battalion commanded by Hauptmann Nowack. (ECPAD)

The Germans Retreat into the Falaise Pocket

In mid-August, Allied commanders demonstrated an inexcusable lapse in communication. Each appeared to be fighting his own war with little concern for his neighboring armies and corps and as a result the Falaise Pocket remained open.

Bradley's first mistake—if indeed it was his and not Montgomery's—was preventing the U.S. XV Corps from proceeding beyond Argentan to link up with the Canadians at Falaise or even beyond, as Patton had suggested. This meant that on the evening of August 13, arriving outside Argentan, Haislip's corps had to stop and wait for the Canadians to arrive, in accordance with Bradley's orders. Even had Montgomery given them the order to advance more quickly toward Falaise, no one could say when the town would be taken, let alone when the British would make their rendezvous with the XV Corps.

A Flakvierling belonging to an unidentified unit in a country lane in Normandy, in August 1944. This is typical of the kind of roads the 7th German Army had to use to flee the Falaise Pocket. (ECPAD)

This Churchill tank has been towed by a rescue vehicle to a field where REME mechanics are ready to get to work. (IWM B9162)

Bradley's Excuses … for Montgomery

Bradley has never clearly explained why he gave the order to halt at Argentan, other than wanting to avoid a collision between the British and American forces. This seems a weak justification, as in order to surround the Germans, the British arm of the pincer actually needed to link up with the American arm.

After the war, Bradley added that he had not thought how the Falaise Pocket could be closed with only four divisions, in the face of 19 German divisions still located east of Argentan at the moment the order was given. But even this justification does not hold water, as, two days later, he reduced the number of divisions to just two, sending Patton toward Chartres and Paris.

However, it has become patently clear that Bradley was simply following Montgomery's instructions and that Eisenhower intervened to save the Anglo-American relationship from deteriorating any further—to the point of collapse, in fact—by ordering Bradley to take the fall for Montgomery's incomprehensible "halt order." It is on record that Bradley and Eisenhower discussed "the Montgomery problem" at some length, but curiously the matter was never taken up directly with Montgomery, in all likelihood to try and preserve the Anglo-American relationship.

U.S. Army historian and 21st Army Group staff officer Dr. Forrest C. Pogue interviewed Montgomery's intelligence officer, Brigadier E. T. "Bill" Williams on May 30 and 31, 1947. Pogue's notes are reasonably indicative:

> Remember [he] was in Freddie's [De Guingand, Montgomery's chief of staff] truck near Bayeux when 2nd French Armored made its swing up and crossed the road towards Falaise. Monty said tell Bradley they ought to get back. Bradley was indignant. We were indignant on Bradley's behalf. De Guingand said, "Monty is too tidy." Freddie thought Bradley should have been allowed to join the Poles at Trun. Monty missed closing the sack. Bradley couldn't understand. Thought we were missing our opportunities over inter-Army rights. However, it should be pointed out that Monty regarded Bradley as under his command; therefore his decision was not made on the basis of inter-Army considerations … Master of tidiness. He was fundamentally more interested in full envelopment than this inner envelopment. We fell between two stools. He [Montgomery] missed his chance of closing at the Seine by doing the envelopment at Falaise. Monty didn't want to do the short hook.

British engineers repurpose a Willys Jeep to take advantage of the Caen–Cherbourg railway line. (IWM B9079)

In Profile:
British Tanks

A British Cromwell from the 8th King's Royal Irish Hussars, Reconnaissance Regiment, 7th Armoured Division, aka the Desert Rats. It is armed with a hedge-cutting device, which, while useless on the Caen plains, would prove invaluable in the Falaise *bocage*.

A Sherman Mark IV (M4A4) from the 11th Armoured Division. The number 50 on a red background designates the HQ of the 29th Armoured Brigade commanded by Brigadier C. B. C. Harvey.

An M5-A1 Stuart from the Polish 10th Armoured Cavalry Brigade. To close the Falaise Pocket, the Poles were sent right into the bottleneck, on Mont-Ormel, where they were faced with German attacks coming from both inside and outside the pocket.

Shermans were used in all the British offensives of August 1944, and were victims of 8.8cm fire, the panzers and the large numbers of mines sewn by the Germans. This Sherman from the 22nd Armoured Brigade has lost its tracks. (IWM B9093)

General Pip Roberts, GOC 11th Armoured Division, in his command car, on August 15, 1944. The British divisions were not engaged on the most important sector of the front—that of Falaise—but instead fought on the Canadians' flanks. (IWM 9183)

Above and facing: Two views of an SdKfz 251 D from the 9th SS Panzer Division Hohenstaufen. The first three registration numbers, only visible here on the rear plate, are the same as on the front. The Pak cannon is also identical and the soldier standing on the hood is recognizable in both images. In the facing photograph the troops have spotted something in the sky—a "Jabo" perhaps. (ECPAD)

Freddie, using my information and his own ideas, persuaded Monty into that with Bradley arguing for it from his angle. Monty didn't want to do it but saw a chance to pull it off after he had pushed Bradley back. In the first stage he was looking toward a grander basis, and he thought, "Hell, those guys are excited; they are spoiling the way we are going." Then Freddie and Bradley favor the short hook. He agrees, but it's already too late. So he misses both opportunities.

This lack of goodwill between the Allies was also evident in Patton's reaction when Bradley ordered him to halt at Argentan. Patton was unconvinced Bradley had been telling the truth:

> I told him [Bradley's chief of staff, General Leven Allen] … it was perfectly feasible to continue the operation [the drive on Falaise]. Allen repeated the order [from Bradley] to halt on the line and consolidate…. I believe that the order … emanated from the 21st Army Group, and was either due to [British] jealousy of the Americans or to utter ignorance of the situation or to a combination of the two. It is very regrettable that the XV Corps was ordered to halt, because it could have gone on to Falaise and made contact with the Canadians northwest of that point and definitely and positively closed the escape gap.

Patton was right on both scores.

The ruined streets of Lisieux, in the rain, at the end of August. A motorcyclist is using his bayonet to affix a sign pointing to a field hospital. For security purposes directions on these makeshift signposts often used the names of unit officers instead of places, so only the troops concerned would know that the directions were aimed at them. (ECPAD)

Dilly-dallying in the German HQ

While the Allies were ignoring each other, the German commanders were ignoring the realities of the terrain, and the situation was getting worse.

At around the time that Bradley—as we have seen, on Montgomery's nonsensical orders—was reining in his divisions, despite being required to close the pincers in a matter of hours, Field Marshal von Kluge, against his better judgement, had still not ordered his troops to retreat east. Instead, he had to prepare a counteroffensive against the Americans, though the direction of this was to change several times due to Patton's advance.

On August 13 at 1800 hours, von Kluge opened communications with Jodl at OKH. He described in great detail the positions reached by the Americans, concluding: "The enemy is trying with all its might to surround the bulk of the 5th Panzer Army and the 7th Army."

In Profile:
German Tank Destroyers and Self-Propelled Artillery

A StuG IV from the 17th SS Panzergrenadier Division Götz von Berlichingen. This division only had StuG IVs on its books: 42 in total.

A heavy reconnaissance armored car, Schwere Panzerspähwagen 234/2 (Puma) from the 130th Panzer Lehr Division. This division was badly mauled during Operation *Cobra*, and played no role in the battle of the Falaise Pocket.

A Sturmgeschütz III G from the 10th SS Panzer Division Frundsberg. The 9th SS Panzer Division Hohenstaufen also had some of these in its inventory.

The contemporary British caption indicated that these two half-tracks belonged to the *Maquis*, the French Resistance, but this is clearly a mistake as the crosses of Lorraine displayed on the flanks of these vehicles identify them as belonging to General Leclerc's 2nd Armored Division, not the *Maquis* who had no such matériel during the summer of 1944. This photograph was taken at Ecouché on August 19, 1944. (IWM B9421)

A Sherman crosses a Bailey bridge in the razed village of Putanges on August 29, 1944, during the final phase of the battle of the Falaise Pocket. (IWM B 9466)

Historians of the battle of Normandy are usually only concerned with the armored divisions, while the infantry divisions—especially those that used horse-drawn transport, like those in the Wehrmacht—are all but forgotten. However, alongside the Tigers, Panthers and other Panzer IVs holding the line were large numbers of infantry. These weary men, photographed in the Lisieux sector in August 1944, belong to the 272nd Infantry Division, pulverized during Operation *Goodwood* and almost annihilated during Operation *Spring*. (ECPAD)

A Canadian self-propelled 25-pounder on a Ram chassis among the ruins of Ecouché on August 19 or 20. The 25-pounder Ram was the approximate equivalent to an American M7 Priest or a British Sexton. (IWM B9460)

He did not ask for authorization for a general retreat, knowing full well that Hitler would refuse it. Showing more diplomacy, he proposed only abandoning positions situated to the west of Flers, in order to free up the panzer divisions for the offensive against the U.S. XV Corps.

On the morning of August 14, Hitler agreed to a limited withdrawal, at the same time ordering a counterattack by Eberbach's armored group on the U.S. XV Corps in the Carrouges–Alençon sector. But the forces available on the ground were lacking in any strength: the 9th Panzer Division had been reduced to a single *kampfgruppe* by its efforts in the Ecouves forest, and the 116th Panzer Division was holding the front at Argentan and had no chance of going on the offensive against an entire U.S. army corps.

Hitler planned therefore to use the divisions holding up part of the British sector, namely the 9th, 10th, and 21st Panzer Divisions. This was wholly unrealistic, as these three divisions were under immense pressure from the enemy in extremely critical sectors—Tinchebray, Vire and Condé-sur-Noireau for the 9th and 10th, Thury-Harcourt for the 21st—and could not easily disengage. Further, were they to withdraw, the front in these sectors would completely collapse.

Nevertheless, von Kluge passed on the order to Eberbach, who sent a response via the "last member of my general staff." The response could not have been any more direct:

> If we want to avoid a total catastrophe, a rapid retreat of the 7th Army under the protection of a flank must be ordered. I will not execute the order of the Supreme Command until the II SS Panzer Corps arrives, and until we are supplied with sufficient food and munitions. Attack impossible before August 16. Success improbable.

At 1137 hours on August 14, half an hour after Sepp Dietrich's divisions had received the order to push south toward the Americans, a new Canadian offensive against Falaise began, throwing all the German plans into jeopardy.

1917 Again

Before focusing on the offensives launched by General Montgomery in the summer of 1944, it is interesting to recall those undertaken by the British in 1917, in World War I. Of course, the presence of tanks and aircraft cannot be seriously compared, but what is similar is perhaps more striking: the lack of imagination, the constant reprise of the same tactic, and the desire to end the conflict on a very straight and "tidy" front line. It was no longer infantry being used as cannon fodder, but armor, while Lancaster bombers replaced artillery. Everything else—the clumsy strategy, the sluggish advance—was almost identical.

Lieutenant-General Brian Horrocks commanded the British XXX Corps. Wounded in North Africa, he had just returned from a long convalescence and was still in poor health, which would take its toll after the ill-fated Operation *Market Garden*. (IWM B9301)

Operation *Tractable* was no different from Operation *Totalize* in terms of its objectives: it always aimed to capture the high ground that loomed over Falaise to the north. This time, the accompanying tanks and armored artillery did not attack in single file, but in large phalanxes up to 250 meters wide. Nocturnal attacks were abandoned in favor of daytime assaults under the cover of artificial smoke screens. The heavy bombers tried once more to prepare the terrain with a massive aerial bombardment.

In Profile:
American Vehicles

An infantry half-track from an unidentified American unit.

A Willys Jeep from C Company, 506th Parachute Infantry Regiment, 101st Airborne Division. The white stars on its bumpers and sides have been painted over with Olive Drab.

A n M8 armored car from the U.S. 82nd Reconnaissance Battalion, 2nd Armored Division.

A Cromwell from the 2nd Northants Yeomanry passes a crowd of French spectators in Flers on August 17. (IWM B9329)

The Germans were unsurprised: on the evening prior to the main assault, an officer from the 8th Canadian Reconnaissance Regiment, carrying the entire Allied operational plans, was shot and killed by the 12th SS Panzer Division, who immediately sent the plans to General Kurt Meyer. Meyer then made use of the cover of night to install 8.8cm cannons in key positions, these guns having already proved so effective against the British.

In an angry missive to his commanders, General Simonds a few days later summed up the disaster:

> On the evening of the 13th August, 1944, an officer of the 8th Cdn Recce Regt, 2 Cdn Inf Div, travelling in a Humber scout car, lost his way and ran into the enemy. He was shot dead, his driver taken prisoner. On searching the body of the officer it was found that he was carrying Copy No. 8 of a 2 Cdn Inf Div Instruction which outlines the whole Corps plan for the attack on the 14th August, 1944.
>
> The German prisoner who gave this information stated that it was his opinion that but for the capture of this order, we would have made a clean break through to FALAISE on the evening of 14th August, 1944. Though the information came into their hands very late, it enabled the enemy to make quick adjustments to his dispositions which undoubtedly resulted in casualties to our troops the following

Tiger 211 from the 102nd SS Heavy Panzer Battalion in the Falaise sector, August 1944. (ECPAD)

The 102nd SS Heavy Panzer Battalion on the move. In front of the Tiger is a captured British Dingo scout car. The two Waffen-SS heavy panzer units were responsible for stopping the Canadian advance into the Falaise Pocket. (ECPAD)

> day, which otherwise would not have occurred, and delayed the capture of Falaise for over twenty-four hours.

Operation *Tractable* began at the designated hour, in a vast cloud of dust. Simonds recorded that the dust raised by the tank charge was as fine as flour, and that it seemed to get in everywhere. First, the ground itself had been pulverized by the bombers, then the artillery barrages had themselves raised a storm of dust and, finally, the tanks finished the job.

The tank crews had received a simple instruction to keep them from losing their way: always advance into the sun. But this implied that they would be able to see the sun, which of course they could not, at least not at the beginning of the assault. And when the dust settled, and they were able to advance with the sun in their eyes, it was incredibly difficult for them to pinpoint the now-backlit enemy positions. In contrast, for the 8.8cm pieces, the enemy was perfectly silhouetted.

Right at the beginning of the attack, Brigadier E. L. Booth, commander of the 4th Armoured Brigade, was killed in his tank leading his troops into battle. The Canadian 3rd Infantry Division pressed on regardless, though they had great difficulty crossing the small

A British column enters Ecouché. The towed antitank 6-pounder was no match against the Tigers. (DITE/USIS)

Laison stream. By late afternoon, the first German line had been vanquished as the infantry swept in behind the tanks as planned: the vanguard of the 3rd Infantry Division was now just 6 kilometers from Falaise.

But the German front did not collapse, because when the first signs of weakness started appearing, German reinforcements quickly plugged the gaps. One such weakness came in the form of two infantry divisions—the 85th and the 89th—which, at the onset of the attack, were to all intents and purposes entirely obliterated by the aerial offensive conducted by 800 Bomber Command aircraft. It is interesting to note in passing that some bombs fell on the Canadian lines, killing over 150 men, an enormous figure given that only 75 men were lost during the entire course of Operation *Totalize*. (This was the other big difference from the offensives of 1917: in 1944, actions were deemed disastrous once losses reached 100 men, while in 1917, this would hardly have raised a general's eyebrow.)

German Counterattacks

As with the previous British assaults, the Germans retaliated with a number of localized counterattacks. These were led once again by the 12th SS Panzer Division and the 102nd Heavy Battalion, equipped with Tigers. The leader of 2nd Company, Ernst Streng, recounts the ensuing battle:

A Tiger from the 102nd SS Heavy Panzer Battalion among the ruins of Falaise. The Tigers were not the only obstacle the Canadians had to face: 8.8cm Flak guns played an even more important role than the tanks. (ECPAD)

A Sherman Firefly outside the Putanges city hall on August 20, 1944. (IWM)

> Our mission was to attempt to repel the tank attacks in the Tournebu sector. Early in the morning, just after 0600hrs, a thick fog, half natural and half artificial, covered the sector. Our infantry was quickly overwhelmed. Suddenly we were in the midst of the enemy infantry, who were trying to surround our HQ company, consisting of just three Tigers. We repelled the waves of the assault by firing from our tanks, but the English had brought in tanks and antitank guns under cover of the hedgerows. The Tiger "Münster" was attacked with close-combat weapons and was hit in the turret, killing and wounding some of the crew.
>
> Schroif and Loritz knocked out an enemy tank apiece, but then the British turned on Loritz's tank, shooting at point-blank range. The first shell hit the turret, probably killing everyone on board; the hatch didn't open. A few seconds later, a second shell ignited the fuel tank. Immense flames leapt into the sky and incinerated the Tiger and its crew, and setting off several explosions. We were filled with such rage and pain at losing one of our best …
>
> Another German counterattack joined us and fought alongside our own feeble forces, but the English defense was too strong. The Tiger "Oberhube," newly repaired, found the front by radio and joined our ranks, then five Panthers, in action to our right, joined us at midday. It was at that time when the enemy's heavy bombers began to attack our sector … in the face of such peril, our grenadiers climbed upon our tanks and we retreated. At 1800hrs, we were sent back to the front line at Hill 184, north of Soulangy. When we arrived, we found our infantry in full retreat, in entire battalions, chased by 12 enemy Shermans. With the last light of the day, we managed to blow up three of them, and our infantry began to dig in.

This testimony is telling: firstly it shows that the Tigers had not been placed on the Canadian line of advance, but in the Tournebu sector to the northwest, to confront a diversionary

In Profile:
German Tanks, Artillery and Vehicles

A Tiger II with a Porsche turret, from the 1st Company, 503rd Heavy Panzer Battalion. Tank number 124 was damaged while towing Tiger number 112: the two tanks were then scuttled and abandoned in the Ticheville sector on August 20, 1944.

A Raupenschlepper Ost. Built by Steyr in Austria, the vehicle weighed 1.5 tons, and was thus too light to carry a heavy load. It was mostly used to tow 7.5cm Paks and 10.5cm howitzers.

A 21cm K18 cannon. The divisions that managed to flee the Falaise Pocket left their heavy ordnance behind, especially cumbersome guns such as this.

attack mounted by the Canadian 2nd Infantry Division. It was not until late afternoon that the Tigers intervened on the Laison and Hill 184, which overlooked the creek.

No sooner had the Canadian assault forces managed to bog down in the marshes in this sector than the *kampfgruppen* from the 12th SS Panzer Division Hitlerjugend appeared. Once again, the attempt at an Allied breakthrough had failed, giving some respite to von Kluge.

The German Retreat Begins

By August 14, 1944, the Germans had lost the Normandy front. Since the Allied landings, they had lost 3,600 officers, 151,000 men and 3,800 *Osttruppen* ("Eastern troops")—almost 160,000 men in total. Numerically, the Allies were even worse off, as their losses totaled over 180,000 men, but the reserves situation was very different. For the Germans, just 30,000 men had been sent to Normandy to restore decimated divisions, and 10,000 more were on their way. On the Allied side, fresh troops were constantly arriving (which could also be said of the Germans, albeit to a far lesser degree), but these reinforcements were sent to troops engaged in continual combat, so there were many, especially in the American units, who were never relieved or rested. The British were not much better off, which explains why the Canadians, then the Polish, were brought in to supplement the weakened British forces.

In the ruins of Lisieux, once a picturesque Norman village, a battered truck drives past two soldiers from the 272nd Infantry Division, who are probably clearing the roads for the vehicles fleeing to the Seine. (ECPAD)

At Lisieux a *feldgendarme* gives directions to a retreating vehicle. According to the road signs, the driver is on his way to the Seine and the military policeman is pointing east. Lisieux was at this time defended by Colonel Burian's *kampfgruppe*, comprising the remnants of the 272nd Infantry Division.

Von Kluge's prospects were not encouraging. As on August 13, Eberbach's *panzergruppe* was but a shadow of its former self: the 1st SS Panzer Division comprised 342 panzer-grenadiers, eight Sturmgeschütz IIIs, 14 Panzer IVs, and seven Panthers; the 9th Panzer Division had 260 panzergrenadiers, and 12 panzers; the 2nd Panzer Division comprised 2,200 men, five Sturmgeschütz IIIs, nine Panzer IVs, and two Panthers. It is understandable then that Hitler rejected the panzer group in favor of the 9th and 10th SS Panzer Divisions and 21st Panzer Division for the attack on the U.S. XV Corps.

Farther east, the German divisions still at Mortain were in a perilous position. The authorization for a limited retreat given by Hitler allowed von Kluge to order a withdrawal in two phases over two nights as far as Flers.

The Canadian attack on August 14 called into question the I SS Panzer Corps' attack on the U.S. XV Corps. The 21st Panzer Division was sent to the front at Falaise to prevent its otherwise imminent collapse. The 10th SS Panzer Division Frundsberg was unable to disengage itself for the offensive, as the Americans were putting severe pressure on the

These Royal Horse Artillery gunners have captured a German car draped in swastika flags, in the middle of the Falaise Pocket, near Argentan, on August 21, 1944. Like many other German vehicles, this car had to be abandoned due to lack of fuel, the roads being completely congested with vehicles coming from the west and south of the *kessel* (the cauldron/pocket). (IWM B9531)

There are no known German photographs from the Falaise Pocket, but this one shows the retreat, and the sign on the store on the right leaves little doubt that it was taken in Normandy. This truck is passing through Brionne, in the Eure region, on its way to the Seine. No fewer than 25,000 German vehicles made it across the river. (ECPAD)

Domfront sector and threatening the front north of the German 7th Army. This left the 9th SS Panzer Division Hohenstaufen to handle the attack on Alençon and Carrouges. Von Kluge knew that the chances of success were growing increasingly slim, and, if he failed, the two German armies in Normandy risked being caught in a trap.

The only alternative was to retreat as quickly as possible out of the pocket via the Falaise–Argentan corridor. At 2330 hours on August 14, von Kluge told Hitler the news.

The Feldmarschall Disappears

Early on August 15, von Kluge left Dietrich's GHQ for the village of Nécy, where he was to attend a meeting with Hausser and Eberbach. Four hours later, any trace of von Kluge had vanished: no radio contact could be established and nobody had seen him for hours.

The same day, which Hitler later referred to as the worst of his life, the Allies landed in Provence on the south coast of France and the situation worsened considerably for the Germans in the Falaise Pocket. The Canadian attacks followed and the desperate efforts of the 12th SS Panzer Division Hitlerjugend were not enough to contain them. In the Domfront sector, the Americans were threatening to break through the last of the German rearguard, and, to the south, Eberbach's armored group lost control of Ecouché. Outside the pocket, the Allies attacked to the southeast of Caen and managed to reach Mézidon and Saint-Pierre-sur-Dives. Someone had to take control of the situation, and with von Kluge nowhere to be found, it was Dietrich who took up the reins. He ordered a retreat beyond the Dives River.

Von Kluge's absence became all the more worrying as according to Gestapo suspicion he was one of the plotters behind the assassination attempt of July 20. No one in Normandy knew of these allegations, but Hitler feared that the field marshal had gone over to the enemy camp to negotiate a separate peace agreement when he heard of the landings in Provence.

This was not the case, as von Kluge was not even aware of the landings. His command car had been destroyed by an Allied fighter-bomber and, caught in the terrible bottlenecks in the Falaise Pocket, the commander-in-chief had to hide out and wait for nightfall.

During the evening, Hitler named Hausser interim head of Army Group B and contacted Model and Kesselring to find a permanent successor to von Kluge. A couple of hours later, von Kluge reappeared.

On August 16 at 1245 hours, he made a phone call to Jodl and gave him his assessment of the situation. Jodl admitted that while retreat was the only sensible option, he thought that it would only be possible if the Falaise bottleneck could be enlarged by an attack directed against Sées from Argentan, as Hitler had ordered Hausser in von Kluge's brief absence.

Von Kluge responded to Jodl directly:

> It doesn't matter how many times the same order is repeated: the troops cannot defeat the enemy. They are not capable and do not have the power necessary to succeed. It would be a fatal error to believe that there is any hope for what cannot be accomplished, and there is no force in the world that can enforce its will with a single order. *That* is the situation.

At Brionne, an SdKfz 251 heads for the Eure, then the Seine, on a rainy August 24. (ECPAD)

This Waffen-SS Horch is leaving Orbec in the rain, and in daylight. (ECPAD)

Jodl responded, saying he understood, and that the Führer would shortly give a directive to this effect.

With this assurance, von Kluge asked General Hans Speidel, his chief of staff, to prepare a draft order for the withdrawal. The 7th Army would begin the retreat the next day, and Hausser would immediately withdraw two divisions from the front, to be replaced by the 5th Panzer Army. The II SS Panzer Corps would be placed under the direct authority of Eberbach's panzer group. The crossing of the Orne, with its very meandering course in the Falaise sector, would be regulated by the general staff of the LVIII Panzer Corps, who would deal with the corridors of communication.

By 1439 hours, Hitler's directive had still not arrived, and von Kluge decided he could wait no longer: he gave the order to retreat. The armies would retreat across the Orne over two nights, the first being that of August 16/17. For the rest, the orders were the same as those provided by Speidel, except that the panzer group also had to withdraw two armored divisions from the pocket as quickly as possible to regroup at Vimoutiers. These two units would serve as reserves for the army group. Eberbach would also try to enlarge the bottleneck by attacking in the Argentan sector.

Two hours later, Hitler's directive finally arrived. In the end, it was more generous than von Kluge had expected, as the Führer accepted the necessity of the retreat to the east as far as the Dives, which is to say, east of the Falaise–Trun line. Hitler also ordered that Falaise should be held at all costs to serve as a cornerstone for the defense, and that Eberbach had to attack from Argentan toward the southeast to widen the bottleneck. Hitler's directive, fortunately for von Kluge, did not contradict anything in the orders von Kluge had already given. The retreat from the Falaise Pocket was all set to begin on the night of August 16/17, at the same time as Falaise fell into the hands of the Canadians. However, because of Bradley's—rather Montgomery's—decision to halt the U.S. XV Corps, the pocket was still not sealed shut, so the 7th Army still had a chance—albeit a slim one—of escape.

Winston Churchill stands with Major-General Brian Horrocks (nearest camera) on a Covenanter tank of 4th/7th Royal Dragoon Guards, 27th Armoured Brigade, to take the salute at an inspection of 9th Armoured Division near Newmarket, Suffolk, May 16, 1942. (IWM H 19765)

In Profile: Lieutenant-General Brian Horrocks

Brian Gwynne Horrocks was born into a military family in India in 1895. After spending some time growing up in Gibraltar, he enrolled in the Royal Military College, Sandhurst where he finished 161st out of a class of 167: by his own admission he was lazy, slovenly and hopeless at drill. He only received his commission—as a subaltern in the Middlesex Regiment—because of the outbreak of World War I, taking part in the British Expeditionary Force's bloody retreat following the battle of Mons.

During the subsequent battle of Armentières in October 1914, his platoon was surrounded, and he was shot and wounded in the abdomen and thigh before being taken prisoner. He was to spend the next four years as a POW—spending much time with Russian POWs learning Russian—before being promoted (in captivity) to lieutenant, awarded the Military Cross (in captivity) and repatriated in December 1918. (He managed to disperse four years' army back-pay on a wild six-week binge in London.)

After the war, Horrocks served with the White Army in Russia in that country's civil war, before being captured by the Red Army while liaison officer with the First Siberian Army. He was released in a prisoner exchange before fighting in the Anglo-Irish War and serving with the British Army of the Rhine in Germany. After competing as a pentathlete in the 1924 Olympics, Horrocks was to spend the interwar years a staff instructor at various military colleges, notably Camberley.

At the outbreak of World War II, he returned to the Middlesex Regiment and was involved in the Dunkirk evacuation of 1940. By March 1942, after service in various Home Counties regiments, Horrocks, now a temporary major-general, took command of the 9th Armoured Division that was transferred to the Western Desert. As corps commander of XIII Corps, Horrocks distinguished himself in Montgomery's North Africa campaign, particularly during the battle of Alamein, before taking over X Corps. In June 1943, he was critically wounded at Bizerte, Tunisia by a strafing German fighter in his chest, lungs, stomach, and intestines. Even after 14 months' convalescence, he never quite recovered (something that was to affect his chances of promotion). Nevertheless, in August 1944, after pleading with Field Marshal Sir Alan Brooke, he was dispatched to Normandy as GOC XXX Corps. This corps, with Horrocks at the helm almost continuously, saw action on The Scheldt, at Arnhem (Operation *Market Garden*), in the Ardennes, and lastly from Northwest Europe into the Third Reich.

Brigadier General James Gavin, CO U.S. 82nd Airborne Division, under Horrocks's command at Arnhem, said later: "He was truly a unique general officer and his qualities of leadership were greater than any I have ever seen. In lecturing at the American service school I stated frequently that General Horrocks was the finest general officer I met during the war, and the finest corps commander." General Eisenhower concurred, referring to Horrocks as "the outstanding British general under Montgomery." The colorful Sir Brian Horrocks died in 1985, a remarkably talented and capable British general.

The Pocket Closes and the Germans Break Out

As the Germans began their retreat from the Falaise Pocket, Bradley made an unexpected decision without warning Montgomery: he was to dispatch Patton ahead to the east, toward the Seine and Paris, thus reducing his forces outside Argentan.

The departure of the U.S. 5th Armored Division and the 79th Infantry Division did not have much of an impact on the front, as the Americans were in static positions and the Germans were not trying to attack, but to retreat as quickly as possible. Some German divisions had already sent their non-essential elements and where possible their artillery eastward, either on their own volition or with the assent of their army corps. Some of these elements even managed to reach the right bank of the Seine without a shot being fired in anger.

At the same time, the II SS Panzer Corps was hastily redeployed in the Vimoutiers sector to oppose the Allied attempts to seal the corridor while Montgomery launched two armored divisions to the southeast.

A view of an Allied depot of German matériel collected from the Normandy battlefields, particularly from the Falaise Pocket. Note at left of the StuG IIIs and other Hummels a number of Panzer IVs in good shape. No Panthers are visible: they are elsewhere in this immense field. (ECPAD)

On August 17, 1944, the Shermans of the 5th Armored Division were already at Chartres, while the German 7th Army began retreating from its positions west of the Orne. The matériel superiority of the Americans was overwhelming, and while the Sherman itself was not as advanced as most German tanks, it was utilized perfectly by the Americans, who benefitted from its speed and reliability to effect deep penetrations, exactly as the Germans had done in May 1940 with panzers considered inferior to the French tanks. (DITE/USIS)

Firm handshakes between American and British military policemen at Tinchebray. In the western part of the Falaise Pocket, the British were in contact with the U.S. First Army, not Patton's Third Army. (IWM B9295)

Luftwaffe infantry prisoners of war rest at the side of a road during the U.S. Third Army's advance. (DITE/USIS)

Model Replaces von Kluge

On August 17, Field Marshal Walter Model arrived in France to replace von Kluge. The latter returned immediately to Germany, where he took his own life, leaving behind a long letter that laid out in detail and with little ambiguity the situation in Normandy. Perhaps surprisingly, in his missive von Kluge showed no bitterness, and neither denied his own role in the failure of the invasion, nor laid blame at the feet of others.

Upon his arrival, Model made a number of important decisions. First, he created four *kampfgruppen* from the remnants of ten divisions, which says much about the state of the 7th Army just before the closure of the Falaise Pocket. Thus, the remnants of the 84th, 85th, 89th and 271st Panzer Divisions formed a *kampfgruppe* of just 1,200 men and eight artillery batteries. Four other infantry divisions were brought together to create a second *kampfgruppe* of similar size, and two other units managed to scrape together a *kampfgruppe* apiece: the 3rd Fallschirmjäger Division (1,500 paratroopers and eight batteries) and the 353rd Infantry Division (2,000 men and six batteries). Model also salvaged 270 tanks as reinforcements, bringing the number of panzers per division to thirty.

While the Germans were reorganizing themselves in the flight from the Falaise Pocket, the Allies decided it was time—at long last—to finish what they had started. The 4th Canadian Armoured Division seized Trun and the Poles reached a position situated just 1 kilometer north of Chambois, cutting off one of the two escape routes for the Germans. To the south, the Americans were also on the offensive, but had not reached Chambois.

On the morning of August 19, the pocket measured 10 kilometers deep by 11 at its widest across the center, where most of the German units were concentrated: six high-ranking staffs, including those of the 7th Army and Eberbach's panzer group; the remnants of six infantry divisions; a division of paratroopers; the 2nd, 116th and 12th SS Panzer Divisions; and a ragtag bevy of stragglers, survivors, engineers and service elements. All were subjected to incessant enemy artillery and aircraft fire.

On the 19th, the 1st Polish Division took Mont-Ormel, right in the center of the German escape corridor. From this dominant position, the Polish troops could fire at will on the German columns fleeing east. In the evening, they reached Chambois and linked up with the U.S. 90th Infantry Division. The Falaise Pocket was closed.

The German Breakout

On August 19, Paul Hausser visited the command post of General Eugen Meindl, commander of the 3rd Fallschirmjäger Division, who considered the visit a bad omen. He greeted Hausser with the words: "I presume that the lid is on the cauldron and we are about to be asked to lift it."

And that is exactly what happened. Throughout the day, Hausser and Meindl drew up a plan of attack, breaking through at Trun and Chambois, capturing Mont-Ormel (or at least part of it) and maintaining a breach to allow the surrounded divisions to escape.

A Panther on the streets of Brionne, in the Eure region. It has escaped the Falaise Pocket, but has not yet reached the Seine. (ECPAD)

On August 21 among the ruins of Argentan, American infantrymen welcome a British Cromwell. Had the British tanks arrived five days earlier, the entire German 7th Army would have been caught in the trap. (IWM B9534)

On August 17, a military policeman searches two German prisoners in the western part of the Falaise Pocket. (IWM B9309)

A short-barreled Panzer IV abandoned in or just outside the Trun–Chambois corridor. The 21st Panzer Division was the only unit issued with this panzer, and had 21 of them alongside 96 later-build Panzer IVs. In August 1944, the 22nd Panzer Regiment had suffered so badly that it was reduced to a single combat group, namely Kampfgruppe von Oppeln Bronikowski, after its commander. As well as being the first panzer division engaged against the Allies on June 6, the 21st Panzer Division was also the last engaged in the battle of the Falaise Pocket on August 21, during which it covered the rear of those units that had already succeeded in fleeing the pocket. (IWM B9707)

These mobile kitchens from a horse-drawn infantry division have been devastated by Allied aircraft in the Chambois sector. (DITE/USIS)

(Estate E. Meindl)

In Profile:
General Eugen Meindl

Eugen Meindl was born in 1892 and joined the army in 1912. He saw action in World War I as a junior officer in various artillery regiments. He continued serving with the artillery after the armistice, first with the Reichswehr, the armed forces of the Weimar Republic, and as from 1935 with the freshly constituted Wehrmacht. He was promoted colonel in November 1938, commanding the 112th Mountain Artillery Regiment in Graz. Prior to transferring to the Luftwaffe in November 1940, he made his first parachute jump—an operational descent—at Narvik in Norway as leader of the "Meindl Group."

During Kurt Student's airborne invasion of Crete in May 1941, Meindl was shot and seriously wounded in the chest, jumping directly into the action at the Platanias Bridge. Taking ten months to recover, he was promoted major-general and took command of the recently created Luftwaffe Division Meindl on the Eastern Front. Six months later he took control of the XIII Air Corps that later became the I Luftwaffe Field Corps.

In 1943 he assumed command of the II Fallschirmjäger Corps on the Western Front, where his paratroopers of the 3rd Fallschirmjäger Division saw considerable action during the Normandy campaign, in the Falaise Pocket in particular. The corps survived the *kessel*, the cauldron, and saw further action at Kleve (Cleves), the Reichswald and at Goch. At the Wesel bridgehead over the Rhine, where he was in command, he advised OKH on March 5, 1945 that it was critical he evacuate his forces. Preempting Hitler's eventual agreement—at considerable risk to himself—he began the evacuation four days prior to Hitler's confirmation, successfully saving the remnants of seven divisions, two panzer units and all their matériel. Meindl was to comment: "All that would float came back again." He led the corps until its surrender at Grossbrekendorf near Schleswig during the first week of May 1945. He only lived a further six years, dying in 1951 at the age of 58.

Two views of the main street in Argentan at the end of the fighting. The devastation was mostly caused by Allied aircraft, but also by the American artillery that pounded the town for several days before it was captured. The Panther that has been abandoned outside the German Employment Office belonged to the 9th Panzer Division. Its 2nd Battalion was equipped with Panthers, though these tanks were usually reserved for the 1st Battalion. The reason for this is that this battalion was actually on loan to the division, rather than being one of its original sub-units. (DITE/USIS)

American troops have just captured a mobile kitchen near Chambois, soup still steaming on the stove. The captured German cook looks glum. The GIs appear fascinated by the manufacture of the *gulaschkanone*, the German nickname "goulash cannon" being a descriptive indication of the kitchen's chimney. (DITE/USIS)

By evening, Hausser returned with a pared-down staff. The infiltration of Allied lines was due to begin at nightfall. At the same time, the 2nd and 9th SS Panzer Divisions would attack from the other side of the cauldron, to help overcome the enemy defense.

After various vicissitudes and losing almost all their matériel, the two divisions of the II Parachute Corps managed to break out of the encirclement, but were unable to hold the door open for those units following.

It was the same for General Hans von Funck's XLVII Panzer Corps, which caught up with the 1st SS Panzer Division Leibstandarte SS Adolf Hitler and the 2nd Panzer Division outside the pocket, thus saving a number of tanks. The 10th SS Panzer Division Frundsberg also managed to escape.

The two corps following—the LXXXIV and LXXIV—were in a more delicate position. The former had only the 12th SS Panzer Division Hitlerjugend under its command, as the two corps tried to break out together. General Kurt "Panzermeyer" Meyer, the commander of the 12th SS Panzer Division, succeeded in escaping with some armored elements, but General Otto Elfeldt, GOC LXXXIV Corps, found himself isolated and, after firing literally his last bullet, was forced to surrender.

On August 20, other divisions (or remnants thereof) managed to escape, but the Canadians arrived to reinforce the Poles so that during the night of 20/21, and the following morning, only individuals and small groups were able to break out to be collected by the II SS Panzer Corps. The exodus slowed to a trickle during the afternoon, and stopped completely

Allied aviation wreaked havoc on the German columns, both motorized and horse-drawn. Among the ruined vehicles are a Citroën truck and a Panzer IV. (IWM B9583)

A Werfer Brigade 9 rocket launcher destroyed by Allied fighter-bombers. Formed in Münster in March 1944, this unit was annihilated in Normandy then reformed in November 1944 under the name of Volkswerfer Brigade 9, fighting in the Ardennes and the Schnee Eifel. (IWM B9593)

Two Panzer IVs abandoned and scuttled by their crews in the Falaise Pocket. Contrary to the myth, the Typhoon's rockets were only marginally effective against the panzers; the vast majority of German tanks found in the pocket had been abandoned by their own crews, rather than destroyed by the Allies. However, non-armored convoys were easy pickings for Allied aircraft. (IWM B9582)

German armor that has managed to flee the cauldron passes through Brionne in the rain. (ECPAD)

Salvation for the fleeing Germans traversing Argentan lay to the east: Trun, and beyond. As for L'Aigle, or what was left of it, the Americans were already there. (IWM B9597)

by 1600 hours. The battle of the Falaise Pocket was over. The armored SS corps fell back to Orbec, 20 kilometers northeast of Vimoutiers.

An Assessment

From a purely strategic perspective, the Falaise Pocket marked the end of the battle of Normandy. The Germans pulled off a spectacular retreat across the Eure region to the Seine, with some 60,000 troops and 25,000 vehicles arriving more or less intact and in varying degrees of fighting ability. But it was a retreat nonetheless, appearing to signal that the Germans had no intention of staying in Normandy, nor even in France.

Falaise was therefore the culmination of the entire Normandy campaign, and a resounding success for the Allies, as defined by the number of tanks in the panzer divisions as at August 21:

- 10th SS Panzer Division: 0
- 12th SS Panzer Division: 10
- 1st SS Panzer Division: no figure available
- 2nd Panzer Division: 0
- 2nd SS Panzer Division: 15
- 9th SS Panzer Division: 20–25
- 116th Panzer Division: 12
- 21st Panzer Division: still fighting

"George [Patton] was already blocking three principal escape routes through Alencon, Sées and Argentan. Had he stretched that line to include Falaise, he would have extended his roadblock a distance of 40 miles. The enemy could not only have broken through, but he might have trampled Patton's position in the onrush. I much preferred a solid shoulder at Argentan to the possibility of a broken neck at Falaise."—Omar Bradley

In the Chambois sector, British Lieutenant Harold Ashby, standing in his Dingo scout car, shows map directions to two American officers, Major Harold Del and Lieutenant-Colonel Earl Diely. (DITE/USIS)

The fighting has just ended in the Falaise Pocket. These Norman farmers are returning home, passing the detritus of the German Army on the road. The burned-out Panther is missing its tracks. (IWM B9595)

This amounts to a total somewhere between 62 and 100 panzers, the higher figure assuming the two divisions that did not report still had 20 panzers apiece. The 9th Panzer Division, not cited, had no panzers whatsoever and the Panzer Lehr no longer existed at all. This means that by the end of the battle of the Falaise Pocket, the panzer divisions had lost 90 percent of their tanks.

These numbers do need to be put into context. Only 220–230 panzers were recovered from the pocket by the Allies, which indicates that a third of the panzers still available to the Germans on or around August 8 managed to escape. Most importantly, the officers and a significant core of personnel had escaped elimination. These men were able to form the basis for the reconstruction of the divisions farther north, where the Allies would once more cross paths with them in The Scheldt, the Ardennes, and at the Rhine.

Of the 110,000–120,000 men who were surrounded, or almost surrounded, around half escaped, 50,000 were captured and 10,000 were killed—a disaster by all accounts. It was not, however, a second Stalingrad, nor the shameful capitulation of an entire army. The German Army was down, but not out.

Tactical Command Langlade of the French 2nd Armored Division was attached to the U.S. 90th Infantry Division on its way to Chambois, arriving there on August 19. It was during this time that this Sherman, named "Montereau," was put out of action. (ECPAD)

Two photographs of a Sherman column from the 1st Polish Armoured Division, charged with positioning itself in the center of the Chambois corridor to close the Falaise Pocket. There, it endured ferocious attacks from the II SS Panzer Corps, which was coming to the aid of the German troops trapped inside the pocket. (IWM B8823 & B8826)

An American corporal surveys a self-propelled rocket launcher destroyed by Allied aircraft. The sheets of paper near the body of a German soldier are probably maps. (DITE)

A Panther in the village of Pierrefitte, August 25, 1944. (IWM B9664)

Over 1,800 dead horses were counted in the Falaise Pocket. (IWM B9668)

General Otto Elfeldt, debonair GOC LXXXIV Corps, shortly after being captured in the pocket, seen here alongside an interpreter. Most senior German generals managed to escape capture.

General Eisenhower inspects the battlefield near Chambois at the end of August 1944. He was satisfied with the scenes of devastation he observed among the German columns, but later wrote that he was aware that most of the panzer divisions had managed to escape despite being greatly weakened. (DITE/USIS)

Summary

After the German failure at Mortain, the Americans realized that the liberation of Brittany could come about far more quickly than they had previously thought. Bradley and Eisenhower therefore decided that Brittany was no longer a priority objective, and instead launched the bulk of Patton's Third Army to the west, to surround the German forces in Normandy.

The advance of the 5th Armored Division was rapid and threatened all the German lines of communication. Attached to it was General Leclerc's 2nd Armored Division, which entered Alençon, the rear base of the German 7th Army. The divisions continued north, up to the edge of Argentan, where they halted on Bradley's orders: the Americans had to wait there for Montgomery, while Patton was authorized to advance farther eastward, toward the Seine and Paris.

Montgomery, for his part, advanced very slowly, despite several offensives with vast resources. General von Kluge tried for several days to get Hitler's authorization for a general retreat beyond the Orne, and then the Dives. By the time he finally received authorization, the Falaise Pocket was almost closed. From August 16 to 20, the German armies withdrew methodically, abandoning huge amounts of matériel as they did so.

Panzer IVs and Panthers were recovered en masse in the Falaise Pocket, as more than 230 panzers were counted after the battle. In comparison, the number of panzers that made it out of the pocket with their panzer divisions was negligible: the most powerful, with 25 operational panzers as of August 21, was the 9th SS Panzer Division Hohenstaufen. The 2nd Panzer Division no longer had any, nor had the 10th SS Panzer Division. As for the Panzer Lehr, it no longer existed as a fighting unit. (ECPAD)

The entire sector between Falaise and Chambois was littered with abandoned and destroyed German vehicles and matériel. (ECPAD)

At the open-air depot, several Panthers await a visit from the scrap merchant. The only German panzer not visible in this series of photographs is the Tiger. These were likely recovered by the French Army, who were more interested in them than in the Panzer IVs. In any case, the number of Tigers would have been far lower than other panzers. (ECPAD)

When the Poles finished closing the pocket at Mont-Ormel, between Trun and Chambois, the Germans launched a counterattack that, while futile, provided enough of a distraction for the majority of the trapped divisions to escape. The units were, however, reduced in the extreme, with no heavy matériel: the ten panzer divisions that fought in Normandy had only 100 panzers between them.

Eisenhower was to comment on the battle:

> The battlefield at Falaise was unquestionably one of the greatest "killing fields" of any of the war areas. Forty-eight hours after the closing of the gap I was conducted through it on foot, to encounter scenes that could be described only by Dante. It was literally possible to walk for hundreds of yards at a time, stepping on nothing but dead and decaying flesh.

On August 23, a new phase of the German retreat began, to the Seine. Would the Allies be able to stop them?

The artillery corner ... (ECPAD)

Afterword

The Normandy campaign ran for almost three months—from D-Day on June 6, 1944 to the liberation of Paris on August 30, 1944—when the plan had envisaged one month maximum. Dogged German resistance, accompanied by the natural defenses of the *bocage* resulted in a cumbersome, and at times clumsy, Allied advance that was often only rescued by overwhelming Allied air power.

In spite of some poor senior leadership, as epitomized by the self-promoting Montgomery, in spite of the inexperience of most of the troops, in spite of the near-disastrous breakdown of the Anglo-American relationship, the Allies were never going to lose the Normandy campaign: their staggering matériel superiority in every arena—particularly in the air—ensured it could never be otherwise. However this was a fact that Hitler never recognized.

Equally, the Germans were never going to win the Normandy campaign. On the back foot before the Allied invasion even began on D-Day, June 6, 1944, their forces split up and scattered piecemeal up and down the Channel in a guessing game of just where the Allies might land, the Atlantic Wall was, like the Siegfried Line, a defensive tactic that should have been consigned to a medieval scrapheap.

Coupled to which was Hitler's strategic ineptitude—the doomed, almost suicidal Operation *Lüttich* a bloody example—that helped seal the Germans' fate in the Falaise Pocket, and thus Normandy. The credit for the campaign ultimately must go to Eisenhower, whose principal role was essentially one of political administration. It was he who managed to keep the Anglo-American relationship on kilter, against all odds and "the Montgomery problem."

The battle of the Falaise Pocket was not a battle in the classic sense, but rather the culmination of the battle for Normandy, the rather messy full stop to a rather messy campaign. It was undeniably an Allied victory and a disastrous German defeat, and although much has been made by historians that the Falaise Pocket was "no Stalingrad," in the context of the Western Front, it was. It paved the way for the conquest of France and the advance into Germany.

Further Reading

Antal, John, *7 Leadership Lessons of D-Day*, Casemate, Philadelphia & Oxford 2017.

Beevor, Anthony, *D-Day: The Battle for Normandy*, Viking, New York 2009.

Buffetaut, Yves, *Allied Armor in Normandy*, Casemate, Philadelphia & Oxford 2018.

Buffetaut, Yves, *German Armor in Normandy*, Casemate, Philadelphia & Oxford 2018.

Guderian, Heinz, *Panzer Leader*, E.P. Dutton & Co., New York 1952.

Hastings, Max, *Overlord: D-Day and the Battle for Normandy*, Simon & Schuster, New York 1984.

Jentz, Thomas, *Panzer Truppen: 1943–1945*, Schiffer Publishing Ltd (U.S.), Atglen 1998.

Keegan, John, *Six Armies in Normandy: From D-Day to the Liberation of Paris, June 6th–August 25th, 1944*, Pimlico, London 2004.

Lefèvre, Eric, *Panzers in Normandy: Then and Now*, After the Battle, Old Harlow 1983.

Leleu, Jean-Luc, *The Canadians at Falaise, 16/17 August 1944*, Ysec, Paris 2007.

Lodieu, Didier, *Normandy 1944: Operation Goodwood* (Men and Battles) (Vols 1 & 2), Histoire et Collections, Paris 2008.

Lucas, James, *Das Reich: The Military Role of the 2nd SS Division 1941–45*, Arms & Armour Press, London 1991.

Mattson, Gregory L., *SS-Das Reich: The History of the Second SS Division 1941–45*, Amber Books, London 2002.

Mellenthin, F. W. von, *Panzer Battles: A Study of Employment of Armor in the Second World War*, University of Oklahoma Press, Oklahoma 1956.

Some of the Germans who got away. (ECPAD)

Index